Dear Customer

May I congratulate you on your wise decision to invest in a matched set of our finest stainless steel cookware? I am sure you were most favorably impressed by the representative pieces you were shown at the time you were offered the opportunity to acquire this handsome merchandise.

But, as you unpack your own complete set, you will naturally be more keenly aware of its truly superior qualities. As you handle each utensil, your first reaction will be that it is really beautiful. Your cookware is the ultimate in design and workmanship. Its polished surfaces will retain their lustre indefinitely with proper usage and minimal care. You can see why we proudly refer to this incomparable cookware as "kitchen jewelry".

No matter how pleased you are with your brand-new cookware at this moment, I know from my own experience that your pleasure will increase as you become acquainted with its many unique features — the self-basting, self-storing covers, the infinite variety of cooking combinations, to name just a few.

The knowledge that you are cooking your food properly, achieving the maximum in nutrition and flavor, with a minimum of attention during the cooking process, will give you a glow of satisfaction that you had the foresight to make this most worthwhile investment in your future.

May I recommend that you read the Use and Care section of your cookbook (pages 5 through 7) before you begin using your cookware? After you have carefully studied the instructions, you will want to complete and return the registration card so that your set of "kitchen jewelry" will be covered by our 50-year guarantee. (For your easy reference, your guarantee is reproduced on the inside back cover of your cookbook.)

And now, be prepared for a lifetime of carefree cooking with your own beautiful new cookware. Should you have any questions, please contact me. I shall be happy to be of service to you.

Sincerely,

Sandra Vee

Customer Relations Division

Geo used Camo
used Camo
Copper-Glo - or Copper
Cleaver - or Zud - (Cleaver)
Sprinkle and rub with
Paper towel,
Don.

Quick and Easy Gourmet Recipes

Happy Birthday Sylvie
From:
Lou & Walt Hopije
2-1-76-

by Hyla O'Connor

The Vollrath Company, Sheboygan, Wisconsin

Editors: Richard Boardman and Ellene Saunders

Photography: Walter Storck

Prepared by the

Creative Editorial and Art Division of

Fawcett Publications, Inc.

67 West 44th Street

New York, New York 10036

Larry Eisinger . . . . .Editor-In-Chief

George Tilton . . . . .Managing Editor

Silvio Lembo . . . . .Art Director

Herbert Jonas . . . . .Art Editor

Elaine E. Sapoff . . . . .Production Editor

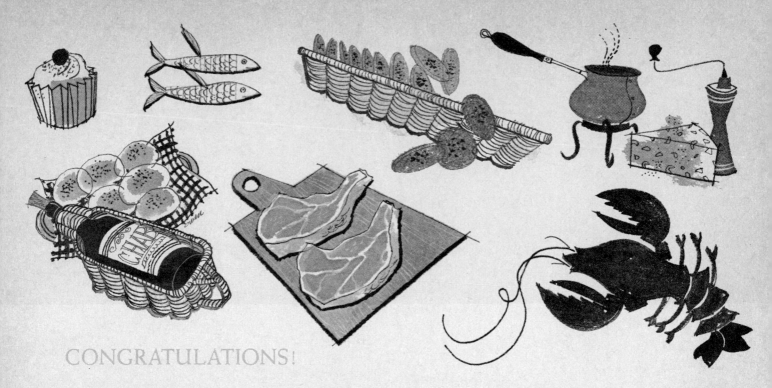

CONGRATULATIONS!

With the acquisition of this cookbook, an unusual concept of cooking foods is at your fingertips. Along with the convenient, easy to prepare recipes are many other helpful hints and suggestions designed to help make your daily meal planning and food preparation as simple as possible.

While no cookbook can guarantee to make you a good cook, by following a few simple rules and doing some pre-meal planning you will increase your chances for a successful meal. First, read the recipe carefully. Make sure you have the utensils or baking pans called for and all the ingredients needed. Measure accurately. Follow cooking or baking instructions to the letter. Be careful of substitutions.

All recipes in this book have been carefully tested and prepared by the author. The author and editors have attempted to provide a quick and easy method for preparing foods that will appeal especially to the beginning cook, yet will also satisfy the exacting requirements of the more experienced cook. It is our sincere wish that you enjoy to the fullest the methods used, and that they make your kitchen tasks easier and your meals more delicious.

THE EDITORS

CONTENTS

HEAT SETTING FOR TOP OF RANGE COOKING 5

CARE AND CLEANING 6

ADDITIONAL EQUIPMENT 7

PASTA 8-13

EGGS 14-17

VEGETABLES 18-41
    Preparation for Cooking • General Cooking Directions • Vegetable Recipes

MEATS 42-73
    Choosing Meat Wisely • General Cooking Directions •
    Beef Recipes • Pork Recipes • Lamb Recipes • Veal Recipes

POULTRY 74-81

PARTY COOKING 82-87

SOUPS 88-93

SEAFOOD 94-99

QUICK BREADS 100-105

DESSERTS 106-117

COOKING TERMS 118-119

A WORD ABOUT BAKING 120

EQUIVALENTS 121

MEAT CHARTS 122-125

Cover Photograph   POT ROAST   FRIED CHICKEN   LOBSTER CANTONESE

Range Settings

GAS RANGE

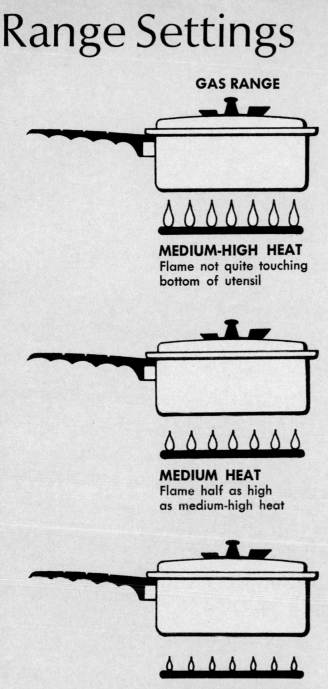

MEDIUM-HIGH HEAT
Flame not quite touching
bottom of utensil

MEDIUM HEAT
Flame half as high
as medium-high heat

LOW OR SIMMER HEAT
Flame barely visible

ELECTRIC RANGE

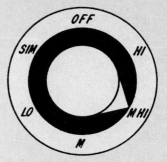

MEDIUM-HIGH HEAT

MEDIUM HEAT

LOW HEAT

SIMMER HEAT

MEDIUM-HIGH HEAT
To preheat utensils for browning meat
To start cooking fruits and vegetables to
allow vapor to escape through vac-control valve
To pan-broil steaks and chops

MEDIUM HEAT
To cook onion and celery when making stews or
sauces
To bring soup stocks to a boil
To brown some steaks, chops, and chicken dishes

LOW HEAT
To cook less tender cuts of meat, such as stews and
pot roasts, after browning
To finish roasting meat after browning
To bake cakes on top of the range

SIMMER HEAT
For long, slow cooking of soups and sauces

Care and Cleaning

...of stainless steel utensils

Wash your utensils the first time in hot, soapy water containing ½ cup vinegar. This removes all traces of manufacturing oils and polishing compounds and makes your utensils ready for use. Rinse in clear hot water; dry well. Care after cooking is as easy as washing your dinnerware.

1. To clean the inside: Empty food from the pan and wash thoroughly in hot water with soap or detergent. Rinse and dry well.
2. To remove residue from dried food or meat drippings, partially fill utensil with hot water; let stand a few minutes. Discard water; loosen food with a wooden spatula, if necessary. Then, rub with a stainless steel cleanser; wash as above.
3. A brownish carbon deposit may appear on the outside of the utensil when cooking over gas. This may be removed by rubbing briskly with a stainless steel cleanser.
4. Utensils should always be thoroughly dried after washing.
5. Golden brown or blue heat tint may result from persistent overheating. Spread stainless steel cleanser on a damp cloth and rub utensil until it is clean. A household cleanser mixed with vinegar can be substituted for stainless steel cleanser.
6. WARNING: Do not use stainless steel or abrasive cleaning pads.
7. Fruits dried by sulphur dioxide method permanently discolor your utensils. We suggest you use fruits dried by the sun or sugar-dried process. All fruit packages are labeled, as required by law, indicating drying processes used.

HELPFUL HINTS

WHEN THIS HAPPENS	WHY IT HAPPENED	WHAT TO DO
Food sticks to bottom of pan.	1. Constant overheating or removing cover during cooking.	1. Soak pan in hot, soapy water. Then clean with stainless steel cleanser.
	2. Range may not be level.	2. Level range.
Pan burns dry.	Constant overheating or removing cover during cooking.	Cool pan before washing. Place in hot, soapy water and clean as above.
Stain on inside of pan.	Constant overheating or action of lime salts in foods.	Remove stain with stainless steel cleanser and damp cloth. Wash and dry.
Golden brown or blue heat tint.	Persistent overheating.	Clean as directed above, in rule 5.
Utensil is scratched.	1. Utensil was cleaned incorrectly.	1. Check cleanser used for cleaning.
	2. A metal spoon may have been used for stirring.	2. Use only wooden spoons for stirring.
	3. Using electric mixer.	3. Do not use electric mixer in pans.

Additional Equipment

You have taken a major step in equipping your kitchen with a complete set of long wearing, durable, good looking pots and pans. However, you will need other basic cooking tools as well. Although you may not want all of them right away, you will find that they are useful for specific tasks.

LARGE ROASTING PAN Buy a large one with a rack, 18½ inches long, 10 inches wide, and 8 inches deep.

ROTARY BEATER For beating sauces, eggs, and cream.

WIRE WHISK Perfect for stirring sauces and gravies to make them lump free. Start with the 8- or 10-inch size.

WOODEN SPOONS For creaming, beating, and stirring. Buy several in assorted sizes for stirring while cooking without scratching the pan, and for mixing foods in bowls.

RUBBER SCRAPERS A kitchen necessity for folding egg whites and whipped cream into mixtures as well as for scraping out bowls and pans.

MIXING BOWLS For all mixing and stirring not done on the range. Buy them in graduated sizes for different jobs.

MEASURING SPOONS For measuring both liquid and dry ingredients. A set of standard measuring spoons comes in ¼ teaspoon, ½ teaspoon, 1 teaspoon and 1 tablespoon sizes.

MEASURING CUPS For measuring dry ingredients. A graduated set of cups is made up of ¼ cup, ⅓ cup, ½ cup, and 1 cup.

GLASS MEASURING CUP For measuring liquids. Buy a glass measuring cup whose rim is above the 1-cup line to avoid spilling. For easier pouring, it should have a pouring lip. The 2-cup and 1-quart sizes are also convenient to have.

CAKE PANS Have two 8- or 9-inch round layer cake pans. Also purchase an 8- or 9-inch square cake pan, good for many things besides baking cakes.

BAKING PANS Buy a loaf pan 9 inches by 5 inches by 3 inches. Useful for loaf cakes and breads, it also fills in if you are short of casseroles. A 9 inch by 13 inch by 2 inch pan is perfect for large loaf cakes and other baking jobs.

PIE PANS Have two 8- or 9-inch pie pans and a 10½-inch juice saver pie pan.

BAKING SHEETS Have at least one for baking cookies and biscuits, and for warming rolls.

ROLLING PIN A necessity for rolling out pie crust. A stocking cover for the rolling pin is often a boon to the beginning cook.

CUTTING BOARD A necessity for slicing and chopping jobs. Many kitchens come equipped with a cutting and chopping board built into the counter top. Have one board for chopping vegetables and onions and another small board for chopping nuts and sweet things, so that you don't have a transfer of odors.

WIRE COOLING RACKS Should be larger than the selected cake pans. Cooling racks are a must when baking cookies, cakes, and rolls.

FLOUR SIFTER For sifting and adding air to flour and for sifting two or more dry ingredients together. A 5-cup size will fit all needs.

PASTRY BRUSH For applying liquids such as oil, milk, or egg whites to the top of piecrusts, breads, or any food that you may wish to cover.

KNIVES A starter set of six should include a chef's knife or French knife, carving knife, meat slicer, utility knife, and two paring knives.

EXTRAS To make cutting, chopping, peeling, and mincing easier, you may want a vegetable parer, a grater, kitchen shears, grapefruit knife, boning knife, and food grinder or chopper.

MORE EXTRAS A long narrow spatula, short wide spatula (called a pancake turner), small strainer, larger strainer or colander, metal tongs, fruit juicer, small reamer for lemon juice, slotted spoon, and can opener.

Pasta

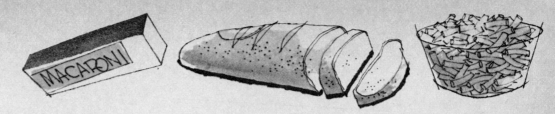

Everyone loves pasta. Just browse through your supermarket and take note of the many varieties—skinny ones, fat ones, round ones, flat ones. Don't limit your cooking to spaghetti and meat balls. Try the other kinds and you will find that a whole new range of recipes will be opened up to you.

BAKED MACARONI AND CHEESE

1 package (8 ounces) elbow macaroni
2 tablespoons butter or margarine
1 small onion, minced
1 tablespoon flour
⅛ teaspoon dry mustard
¾ teaspoon salt
¼ teaspoon Worcestershire sauce
  Dash of pepper
2 cups milk
½ pound sharp Cheddar cheese, grated

1. Heat oven to 400°F.
2. Cook macaroni according to package directions. Drain in colander. Set aside.
3. Melt butter in a saucepan over medium heat. Add onion and cook for 1 minute. Stir in flour. Remove from heat and stir in dry mustard, salt, Worcestershire sauce and pepper. Slowly stir in milk. Cook over medium-low heat, stirring constantly, until mixture is smooth and comes to a boil. Add cheese and stir over low heat until cheese is melted and sauce is smooth.
4. Combine sauce and macaroni. Turn into a lightly greased 1½-quart casserole.
5. Bake about 20 minutes or until hot and bubbly.
6. Makes 4 to 6 servings.

FAMILY FAVORITE MACARONI

⅓ cup butter or margarine
¼ pound fresh mushrooms, sliced
1 cup chopped onions
¼ cup flour
1 can (1 pound) tomatoes
1 cup milk
¼ teaspoon rosemary
1 teaspoon salt
1 package (8 ounces) elbow macaroni
½ pound American cheese
1 can (9¼ ounces) tuna
¼ cup grated Parmesan cheese
¼ cup buttered bread crumbs

1. Heat oven to 400°F.
2. Melt butter in a saucepan over medium heat. Add mushrooms and onions and cook until limp but not browned. Stir in flour. Remove from heat. Stir in tomatoes, mashing tomatoes against the side of the saucepan with the back of a wooden spoon. Cook over medium heat, stirring constantly, until mixture thickens slightly. Remove from heat.
3. Stir in milk, rosemary and salt. Return to heat and cook, stirring constantly, until mixture comes to a boil and thickens.
4. Cook macaroni according to package directions. Drain in colander.
5. Combine onion-tomato mixture with macaroni, American cheese and tuna. Pour mixture into a shallow 2-quart casserole.
6. Combine Parmesan cheese and bread crumbs. Sprinkle over top of casserole.
7. Bake about 25 to 30 minutes or until hot and bubbly.
8. Makes 6 servings.

MACARONI PORK CASSEROLE

2 cups elbow macaroni
2 tablespoons butter or margarine
¼ cup chopped onion
2 cups roast pork, cut in cubes
1 can (11 ounces) condensed Cheddar cheese soup
½ cup milk
¼ cup dark seedless raisins
1 teaspoon salt
⅛ teaspoon pepper
1 tablespoon minced parsley

1. Heat oven to 350°F.
2. Cook macaroni according to package directions. Drain in colander. Set aside.
3. Melt butter in a saucepan. Add onion and cook until tender but not browned. Combine onion, macaroni, pork, cheese soup, milk, raisins, salt, pepper and parsley. Turn mixture into a 2-quart casserole.
4. Bake 20 minutes or until mixture is hot and bubbly.
5. Makes 4 servings.

MOUNTAINEERS' MACARONI AND TUNA

2 cups elbow macaroni
2 tablespoons butter or margarine
2 tablespoons flour
2¼ cups milk
½ teaspoon salt
¼ teaspoon pepper
½ teaspoon caraway seed
½ cup chopped ripe olives
2 cans (6½ to 7 ounces each) chunk-style tuna, drained
1 cup grated Swiss cheese

1. Heat oven to 375°F.
2. Cook macaroni according to package directions. Drain in colander. Set aside.
3. Melt butter in a saucepan over medium heat. Stir in flour. Remove from heat and gradually stir in milk. Return to heat and cook, stirring constantly, until sauce comes to a boil and thickens. Add salt, pepper and caraway seed.
4. In a large mixing bowl combine macaroni, olives, tuna and sauce. Mix lightly but thoroughly. Pour mixture into a 2-quart baking dish. Sprinkle with Swiss cheese.
5. Bake about 25 minutes or until heated through and bubbly.
6. Makes 4 to 6 servings.

COMPANY CASSEROLE

1 package (8 ounces) egg noodles
1 tablespoon butter or margarine
1 pound ground chuck
2 cans (8 ounces each) tomato sauce
1 package (8 ounces) creamed cottage cheese
1 package (8 ounces) cream cheese, softened
¼ cup sour cream
⅓ cup minced green onions
1 tablespoon minced green pepper
Salt and pepper

1. Heat oven to 375°F.
2. Cook noodles according to package directions. Drain in a colander. Set aside.
3. Meanwhile melt butter in skillet over medium-high heat. Add chuck and cook, stirring with a fork, until meat has lost its red color and is lightly browned. Stir in tomato sauce. Simmer 2 minutes and remove from heat.
4. Combine cottage cheese, cream cheese, sour cream, onions and green pepper. Mix together and season to taste.
5. Spread half of the noodles in the bottom of a 2-quart casserole. Cover with cheese mixture and top with remaining noodles.

Pour meat-tomato mixture over top of casserole.
6. Bake 45 minutes or until hot and bubbly.
7. Makes 4 to 6 servings.

EGG NOODLE BAKE

1 large onion, chopped
2 cloves garlic, halved
2 tablespoons salad oil
1 quart tomato juice
1 can (6 ounces) tomato paste
1½ teaspoon salt
¾ teaspoon Italian seasoning
⅛ teaspoon pepper
1 medium green pepper, diced
1 package (1 pound) wide egg noodles
2½ cups cooked diced lamb or beef
1 package (8 ounces) creamed cottage cheese
½ pound Mozzarella cheese, sliced

1. In a saucepan, cook onion and garlic in oil until onion is tender, but not browned. Discard garlic. Add tomato juice, tomato paste, salt, Italian seasoning and pepper. Cover with vac-control valve closed. Reduce heat and simmer 30 minutes. Add green pepper and continue cooking for 15 minutes.
2. Heat oven to 350°F.
3. Cook egg noodles according to package directions. Drain in colander. Combine with diced meat and tomato sauce.
4. Pour mixture into a 13- by 9- by 2-inch baking pan or large shallow casserole. Spread cottage cheese over top. Cover with Mozzarella cheese slices.
5. Bake 20 minutes or until cheese melts and mixture is hot and bubbly.
6. Makes 8 servings.

TURKEY-HAM CASSEROLE

½ cup butter or margarine
1 cup chopped onion
¾ cup diced green pepper
1 can (4 ounces) pimiento, diced
¾ cup sliced ripe olives
½ teaspoon salt
1 teaspoon oregano
1½ cups diced cooked turkey
1½ cups diced cooked ham
2½ cups cooked egg noodles
2 cups canned applesauce
2 tablespoons melted butter

1. Heat oven to 375°F.
2. Melt butter in skillet over medium heat. Add onion and green pepper and cook until limp but not browned. Add pimiento, olives, salt and oregano. Remove from heat.

3. Place turkey pieces in bottom of a buttered 2-quart casserole. Place ham pieces on top of turkey. Top with 1½ cups of the cooked noodles. Spread onion-green pepper mixture over top.
4. Spoon apple sauce over top of onion layer. Toss remaining noodles with melted butter. Place in a ring around edge of casserole.
5. Bake 25 to 30 minutes or until piping hot and bubbly.
6. Makes 6 to 8 servings.

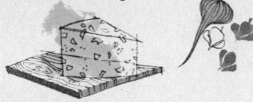

TURKEY TETRAZZINI

¼ cup butter or margarine
½ cup sliced onions
¼ cup flour
1 teaspoon salt
¼ teaspoon pepper
½ teaspoon poultry seasoning
½ teaspoon dry mustard
2 cups milk
½ cup shredded sharp Cheddar cheese
2 tablespoons chopped pimiento
1 can (4 ounces) mushrooms, stems and pieces
1 package (7 ounces) thin spaghetti, cooked and drained
2 cups diced cooked turkey
⅓ cup shredded sharp Cheddar cheese

1. Heat oven to 400°F.
2. Melt butter in a medium saucepan. Add onions and cook gently until onion is tender but not browned. Blend in flour, salt, pepper, poultry seasoning and dry mustard. Cook 1 minute.
3. Remove saucepan from heat and stir in milk. Return to heat and cook, stirring constantly, until mixture thickens and comes to a boil. Add ½ cup shredded cheese and pimiento. Continue cooking until cheese is melted.
4. Remove sauce from heat and stir in mushrooms and mushroom liquid.
5. Place a layer of cooked spaghetti in a 2-quart casserole. Cover with a layer of turkey and a layer of sauce. Repeat process and finish with a layer of spaghetti. Sprinkle ⅓ cup Cheddar cheese over top of casserole.
6. Cover casserole and bake about 20 minutes or until cheese melts and mixture is piping hot.
7. Makes 6 servings.

CHIPPED BEEF-NOODLE CASSEROLE

2 cups cooked noodles
2 hard-cooked eggs, diced
2½ ounces chipped or dried beef, shredded
2 tablespoons butter
¼ cup finely chopped onion
2 tablespoons flour
1 cup milk
¼ cup dry white dinner wine
1 teaspoon prepared mustard
1 teaspoon Worcestershire sauce
⅓ cup grated Cheddar cheese

1. Heat oven to 375°F.
2. Combine noodles, eggs, and beef in a bowl.
3. Melt butter in a skillet over medium heat. Add onion and cook, stirring, until onion is soft but not browned.
4. Remove skillet from heat and stir in flour. Slowly stir in milk and blend until smooth.
5. Cook over medium heat, stirring constantly, until sauce begins to thicken.
6. Add wine, mustard and Worcestershire sauce to mixture in skillet and cook for about 3 minutes.
7. Combine sauce with noodle mixture and blend well. Taste and add more salt and pepper, if necessary.
8. Turn noodle mixture into buttered casserole.
9. Top with grated cheese.
10. Bake 25 to 30 minutes or until mixture is hot and bubbly.
11. Makes 4 servings.

HAM CASSEROLE

1½ cups diced cooked ham
2 tablespoons chopped onion
⅛ teaspoon tarragon
2 tablespoons butter or margarine
1 can (10½ ounces) condensed cream of chicken soup
½ cup water
1½ cups cooked narrow noodles
½ cup cooked French style green beans
2 tablespoons fine dry bread crumbs
½ clove garlic, minced

1. Heat oven to 350°F.
2. Cook ham, onion and tarragon in 1 tablespoon butter until ham is lightly browned and onion is tender.
3. Remove from heat and stir in soup, water, noodles and green beans.
4. Pour into buttered 1-quart casserole.
5. In a small skillet lightly brown the bread crumbs and garlic in remaining tablespoon of butter. Sprinkle over top of casserole.
6. Bake 30 minutes or until hot and bubbly.
7. Makes 4 servings.

GREEN NOODLES EN COQUILLE

3 cups green noodles, uncooked
¼ cup butter
¼ cup flour
1 teaspoon salt
¼ teaspoon Tabasco
2½ cups milk
1 cup diced sharp Cheddar cheese
¼ cup grated Parmesan cheese
3 hard-cooked eggs, halved

1. Heat oven to 350°F.
2. Cook noodles according to package directions. Drain and rinse. Set aside.
3. Melt butter in a saucepan. Stir in flour, salt and Tabasco. Remove from heat and stir in milk.
4. Cook over medium heat, stirring constantly, until mixture is smooth and slightly thickened. Add Cheddar cheese and Parmesan cheese and stir until cheese is melted.
5. Combine noodles and sauce. Pour mixture into a 1½-quart casserole.
6. Bake 30 minutes. Top casserole with egg halves during last 5 minutes of baking.
7. Makes 6 servings.

* * *

SPAGHETTI SAUCE

1 pound ground beef
1 cup finely chopped onion
2 tablespoons shortening
3 cans (8 ounces each) tomato sauce
1 can (6 ounces) tomato paste
1½ teaspoons salt
⅛ teaspoon pepper
½ teaspoon garlic salt
1 teaspoon paprika
½ teaspoon basil
¼ teaspoon marjoram
¼ teaspoon parsley flakes
⅛ teaspoon celery salt
¼ teaspoon dry mustard
2 teaspoons Worcestershire sauce
1 package (1 pound) spaghetti

1. Heat skillet over medium-high heat. Place ground beef, chopped onion and shortening in hot skillet. Cook, stirring with a fork, until meat is broken up and has lost its red color. Pour off excess drippings.
2. Add tomato sauce, tomato paste, seasonings and Worcestershire sauce. Cover with vac-control valve closed. Lower heat and simmer 2 hours, stirring occasionally.
3. Cook spaghetti according to package directions. Drain in colander.
4. Pour spaghetti into a serving dish or platter. Top with spaghetti sauce.
5. Makes 4 to 6 servings.

MEAT BALLS AND SPAGHETTI

2 pounds ground beef
½ cup grated Cheddar cheese
2 teaspoons caraway seeds
2 tablespoons snipped parsley
1 green pepper, chopped
2 eggs, slightly beaten
4 teaspoons salt, divided
½ teaspoon pepper
2 tablespoons salad oil
1 clove garlic
1 large onion, chopped
2 cans (No. 2½) tomatoes
2 cans (6 ounces) tomato paste
½ teaspoon sugar
2 bay leaves
Hot cooked spaghetti
Grated Parmesan cheese

1. Combine beef, cheese, caraway seeds, snipped parsley, green pepper, eggs, 2 teaspoons of the salt, and pepper. Mix thoroughly. Shape into little meat balls, about 1 inch in diameter.
2. Heat salad oil in skillet over medium-high heat. Put garlic in hot oil. Brown meat balls on all sides in hot oil. Add chopped onion and cook until tender, about 5 minutes.
3. Add tomatoes, tomato paste, sugar, remaining 2 teaspoons salt and bay leaves. Cover tightly and simmer very slowly about 1½ hours. Stir occasionally.
4. Serve meat balls and sauce over hot cooked spaghetti. Sprinkle with grated Parmesan cheese.
5. Makes enough sauce for 8 servings.

ROSY SPAGHETTI

1 package (8 ounces) spaghetti
1 package (3 ounces) cream cheese, softened
2 tablespoons butter or margarine
½ teaspoon salt
¼ teaspoon Worcestershire sauce
Dash of pepper
1½ cups tomato juice
2 tablespoons chopped parsley

1. Heat oven to 350°F.
2. Cook spaghetti according to package directions. Drain in a colander.
3. Combine spaghetti, cheese, butter, salt, Worcestershire sauce and pepper. Toss until cheese and butter are melted. Stir in tomato juice and parsley.
4. Turn into a 1-quart baking dish. Cover and bake 30 minutes.
5. Makes 4 to 6 servings.

SPAGHETTI SAUSAGE CASSEROLE

1 package (8 ounces) spaghetti
2 tablespoons butter or margarine
2 tablespoons flour
1 teaspoon salt
⅛ teaspoon pepper
¼ teaspoon dry mustard
2 cups milk
2 cups grated sharp Cheddar cheese
⅓ cup chopped green pepper
1 pound sausages, browned

1. Heat oven to 375°F.
2. Cook spaghetti according to package directions. Drain in colander. Set aside.
3. Meanwhile, melt butter in a saucepan over medium heat. Stir in flour, salt, pepper and dry mustard. Remove from heat. Gradually stir in milk. Return to heat and cook, stirring constantly, until mixture boils. Stir in cheese and green pepper and cook until cheese is melted and sauce is smooth.
4. Combine sauce with spaghetti and toss well. Pour half the mixture into a 2-quart baking dish. Arrange half the sausages on top of spaghetti. Top with remaining spaghetti and sausages.
5. Cover baking dish and bake 20 minutes or until mixture is hot and bubbly.
6. Makes 4 servings.

CALIFORNIA LASAGNA

2 tablespoons salad oil
1 pound ground beef
1 large onion, chopped
2 cloves garlic, minced
1 teaspoon basil
1 teaspoon oregano
2 teaspoons salt
1 can (1 pound, 14 ounces) tomatoes
1 can (6 ounces) tomato paste
¾ cup dry red table wine
½ pound lasagna noodles
2 pound Mozzarella cheese, sliced
½ cup grated Parmesan cheese

1. Heat salad oil in skillet over medium-high heat. Add beef and cook, stirring with a fork, until meat is broken up and has lost its red color. Add onion and cook until onion is transparent. Add garlic, basil, and oregano and cook for a few minutes, stirring constantly. Add salt, tomatoes, tomato paste and wine. Cover with vac-control valve closed. Lower heat and simmer 30 minutes. Remove cover and simmer 30 minutes, stirring occasionally.
2. Cook lasagna according to package directions. Drain and rinse thoroughly.
3. Heat oven to 350°F.
4. Spread a small amount of the sauce in a 12- by 9- by 3-inch baking dish. Cover sauce with a layer of noodles. Cover with some sauce, a few slices of Mozzarella and a sprinkle of Parmesan cheese. Repeat process until noodles, sauce and cheese are used.
5. Bake 30 to 45 minutes or until hot and bubbly and the cheese is melted.
6. Makes 6 to 8 servings.

QUICK LASAGNA

1½ pounds ground beef
1 envelope (1¾ ounces) onion soup mix
3 cans (8 ounces each) tomato sauce
1 cup water
1 package (8 ounces) lasagna noodles
½ pound Mozzarella cheese, sliced

1. Heat skillet over medium-high heat. Add beef and cook, stirring with a fork, until meat is broken up and has lost its red color. Stir in onion soup mix, tomato sauce and water. Bring to a boil. Cover with vac-control valve closed. Reduce heat and simmer 15 minutes.
2. Cook noodles according to directions on package. Drain well and let stand in cool water for easier separating.
3. Heat oven to 400°F.
4. In a 2-quart oblong baking dish, alternate layers of noodles, meat sauce and cheese, ending with cheese.
5. Bake 15 minutes or until hot and bubbling.
6. Makes 6 to 8 servings.

FETTUCINE ALLA ROMAN

½ pound fettucine
¼ cup butter, at room temperature
½ cup grated Parmesan cheese
¼ cup heavy cream, heated
½ cup cooked peas, hot
⅓ cup finely shredded prosciutto
Freshly ground black pepper

1. Before cooking fettucine, heat a serving dish and have a strainer or colander ready to drain fettucine.
2. Place fettucine into boiling salted water and cook according to package directions. Do not overcook.
3. Place butter in heated serving dish. Pour cooked fettucine into strainer or colander. Pour moist fettucine into serving dish and toss quickly with melted butter.
4. Add cheese, cream, peas and prosciutto and continue tossing. Serve immediately on heated plates with a seasoning of freshly ground black pepper on top.
5. Makes 2 large or 4 small servings.

Eggs

Eggs are not only the great American breakfast dish, but also make excellent lunch and dinner dishes. Buy eggs only in stores where they are kept under refrigeration, and keep them refrigerated at home. Their shell color does not affect flavor, nutritive value, or cooking performance. Grades AA and A are especially desirable for cooking in the shell, poaching, and frying. Grades B and C are very good for scrambling, baking, and general cooking. Most standard recipes are based on the use of large- or medium-sized eggs.

FRIED EGGS

1. Melt butter in skillet over medium heat until bubbly. Reduce heat to low.
2. Break egg into a cup; lower cup close to butter in skillet; slide egg into skillet. Repeat, arranging eggs side by side, until the desired number of eggs are in the skillet.
3. Cover and cook just until white is set or to the desired degree of firmness.
4. Sprinkle with salt and pepper.
5. Remove eggs with pancake turner, tilting them against side of skillet to drain well.
6. Serve alone or with bacon, ham slices, or sausage.

SOFT-COOKED EGGS

1. Have unshelled eggs at room temperature. Place in a saucepan and add enough cold water to cover eggs by at least 1 inch.
2. Cover saucepan and bring to a rapid boil.
3. Remove from heat or, if cooking more than 4 eggs, let stand over very low heat. Let stand, covered:
   Very soft-cooked eggs..................2 minutes
   Medium soft-cooked eggs....3 to 3½ minutes
   Firm soft-cooked eggs........about 4 minutes
4. Let cold water run over eggs as soon as cooking time is up to stop further cooking and make them easier to handle.
5. Serve immediately in egg cups.

HARD-COOKED EGGS

1. Have unshelled eggs at room temperature. Place in a saucepan and add enough cold water to cover by at least 1 inch.
2. Cover saucepan and bring to a rapid boil.
3. Remove from heat and let stand, covered, 15 minutes.
4. Let cold water run over eggs as soon as cooking time is up. This makes shells easier to remove and prevents dark surface on egg yolks.
5. To remove shells, tap entire surface of each egg to crackle it. Roll egg between hands to loosen shell, then peel, starting at large end. Dipping eggs into cold water will help ease off shell.

POACHED EGGS

1. Place 1 inch water in skillet. Place utility rack in skillet. Bring water to a boil.
2. Butter utility cups. Place in rack in poacher. Break each egg in a small dish or cup and slip into utility cup.
3. Cover; reduce heat to low and let stand 3 to 5 minutes, or until white is firm and a white film covers the yolk.
4. Serve each egg on a slice of hot buttered toast.

BAKED EGGS

1. Heat oven to 325°F.
2. Butter individual shallow baking dishes or custard cups.
3. Carefully break 1 or 2 eggs in each cup. Sprinkle with salt, pepper and paprika. Dot with butter.
4. Bake, uncovered, 12 to 18 minutes or until of desired degree of doneness.
5. Serve in dishes, garnished with snipped chives or parsley.
6. For a luncheon dish, place bits of cooked bacon, shredded cheese, or cooked ham in bottom of baking dish.

SCRAMBLED EGGS

8 eggs
¾ teaspoon salt
⅛ teaspoon pepper
¾ cup milk or light cream
2 tablespoons butter or margarine

1. Break eggs into a mixing bowl. Add salt, pepper, and milk. With a fork, mix thoroughly.
2. Melt butter in large skillet, tilting skillet so that bottom and sides are covered.
3. Pour in eggs and reduce heat to low.
4. Cook slowly, gently lifting from bottom and sides with a wooden spoon as mixture sets, so liquid can flow to bottom.
5. Cook until set but still moist and slightly underdone.
6. Remove from heat and serve immediately.
7. Makes 4 servings.

PUFFY CHEESE OMELET

6 eggs
½ teaspoon salt
   Dash of pepper
½ cup of grated Cheddar cheese, divided
1 tablespoon butter

1. Separate eggs into 2 large bowls.
2. Beat egg whites with rotary beater until stiff but not dry.
3. Using same beater, without washing, beat egg yolks about 2 minutes. Remove beater and stir in salt, pepper and ¼ cup grated cheese.
4. Pour yolk mixture over egg whites and fold into egg whites with a rubber scraper, until almost all the white is dispersed.
5. Heat butter in large skillet over low heat.
6. Turn mixture into skillet and cook over low heat, about 5 minutes. As eggs cook, lift outer edges towards center, so that uncooked mixture goes to bottom of pan. Cook until eggs are browned on bottom and top has puffed up but is not dry.
7. Sprinkle with remaining cheese. Place on broiler rack about 4 inches from source of heat and broil until top is puffy and lightly browned.
8. Cut into pie-shaped wedges for serving.
9. Makes 4 to 6 servings, depending on appetites.

MUSHROOM POACHED EGGS

2 tablespoons butter or margarine
½ cup minced onions
1 can (10½-ounces) condensed cream of mushroom soup
⅓ cup milk
6 eggs
3 English muffins, split
6 thin slices cooked ham

1. Melt butter in large skillet. Add onions and cook over medium heat just until onions are tender but not browned.
2. Blend in soup and milk and heat to boiling. Reduce heat to low.
3. Carefully break eggs into a saucer, then slide into sauce, one by one, side by side.
4. Cover skillet and cook 7 to 10 minutes or until eggs are cooked to taste.
5. While eggs are cooking, toast muffins and butter.
6. Place a muffin half on a plate, top with 1 slice of ham. Cover with 1 egg and some of the sauce.
7. Makes 6 servings.

EGGS BENEDICT

4 slices cooked ham, about ¼ inch thick
2 English muffins
4 poached eggs
   Quick Hollandaise Sauce
   Parsley

1. Brown ham slices in skillet over medium heat.
2. Split English muffins in half. Toast and butter lightly.
3. Arrange ham on top of muffins. Top each with a poached egg. Cover with Hollandaise sauce. Garnish with parsley.
4. Makes 4 breakfast servings, or 2 dinner servings.

QUICK HOLLANDAISE SAUCE

½ cup butter or margarine
1 egg
2 tablespoons lemon juice
¼ teaspoon salt
   Few grains cayenne pepper

1. Melt butter in top of double boiler over hot, *not boiling,* water.
2. Add egg, lemon juice, salt and cayenne. Beat with rotary beater or wire whisk until mixture is thick.
3. Remove at once from hot water. Serve over eggs.
4. Makes ¾ cup sauce.

Note: Can be used over many cooked vegetables.

CREAMED EGGS

3 tablespoons butter or margarine
1 tablespoon minced onion
3 tablespoons flour
½ teaspoon salt
   Pinch of pepper
1 teaspoon Worcestershire sauce
2 cups milk
6 hard-cooked eggs
1 tablespoon snipped parsley

1. Melt butter in saucepan. Add onion and simmer, stirring, until onion is tender.
2. Remove from heat. Stir in flour, salt, pepper, and Worcestershire sauce. Slowly stir in milk.
3. Cook over low heat, stirring constantly, until mixture thickens and comes to a boil.
4. Peel eggs. Cut into slices, halves or quarters. Add to sauce and heat over very low heat.
5. Serve over toast with parsley sprinkled on top.
6. Makes 4 to 6 servings.

6 hard-cooked eggs
¼ cup finely chopped celery
1 tablespoon mayonnaise
1 teaspoon prepared mustard
6 slices cooked ham
1 can (10½ ounces) cream of mushroom soup
⅓ cup milk
½ cup grated Cheddar cheese
¼ cup crushed potato chips
Sliced stuffed olives

1. Heat oven to 350°F.
2. Slice eggs in half lengthwise. Carefully remove egg yolks with a spoon. Place in a bowl and mash well with a fork. Add celery, mayonnaise and mustard and blend well. If mixture is not moist enough, add a little more mayonnaise.
3. Refill egg whites with mixture. Put two halves together. Wrap each egg in a ham slice. Place eggs in shallow baking dish, fold side down.
4. Combine mushroom soup and milk and blend well. Pour over ham rolls. Sprinkle with grated cheese and potato chips.
5. Bake about 30 minutes or until sauce is bubbly.
6. Makes 6 servings.

CHEESE SOUFFLE

4 eggs
3 tablespoons butter or margarine
¼ cup flour
½ teaspoon salt
Speck cayenne pepper
1 cup milk, warmed
¼ pound process sharp Cheddar cheese, grated

1. Heat oven to 300°F.
2. Separate eggs, putting whites in a large bowl and yolks in a smaller bowl.
3. Melt butter in a saucepan over low heat.
4. Remove from heat and stir in flour, salt, and pepper. Slowly stir in warm milk until mixture is smooth.
5. Cook over low heat, stirring constantly, until mixture is smooth and thick.
6. Add cheese and stir until mixture is smooth and cheese is completely melted. Remove from heat.
7. Beat egg yolks with a fork. Stir a little of the hot cheese sauce into the yolks. Slowly stir this mixture back into cheese sauce in saucepan. Scrape all mixture from bowl into pan with a rubber scraper.
8. With an electric mixer or rotary beater, beat egg whites until stiff but not dry. Pour cheese sauce into egg whites. Fold in with a rubber scraper until no large areas of egg whites remain.
9. Pour mixture into an ungreased 1½-quart casserole with straight sides (A special soufflé dish is very nice to have here)
10. Bake uncovered, 1 hour and 15 minutes. *Don't open oven door while souffle is baking. Wait.*
11. Makes 4 servings.

SHRIMP EGG-FOO-YONG

1 cup drained canned bean sprouts
⅔ cup chopped onions
1 cup cleaned, cooked shrimp
6 eggs
Salad oil
2 teaspoons soy sauce
1 teaspoon cornstarch
1 teaspoon sugar
¾ teaspoon salt
½ cup water

1. Combine bean sprouts and onions in a bowl. If shrimp are large, cut in small pieces. Add to bean sprout mixture.
2. Break eggs into a bowl and beat well with a fork. Stir in bean sprout mixture.
3. In a small saucepan combine soy sauce, cornstarch, sugar, and salt. Stir in water. Cook over low heat, stirring, until thickened. Keep warm over very low heat.
4. Heat salad oil in a skillet over medium heat. Put about ¼ cup of egg mixture in skillet as for pancakes. Fry on one side until golden brown, turn and brown other side. Arrange on a hot platter and keep warm while frying remaining mixture.
5. Cover with heated sauce and serve hot.
6. Makes 3 or 4 servings.

Cauliflower with Cheese Sauce
Golden Nugget Brussels Sprouts

Vegetables

Vegetables are always in season! Your local market has them in abundance all year round, fresh and frozen. When the ones grown in your own locality are available, your choice is even more spectacular. Properly cooked, they will be crisply tender, perfectly seasoned. Everyone will ask for more.

CARE OF FRESH VEGETABLES

1. Buy only the freshest vegetables available.
2. As soon as vegetables are in the kitchen, remove any withered leaves, discoloration or indication of decay.
3. Store onions, potatoes, garlic, winter squash and other less perishable vegetables (so-called dry vegetables) in a container where cool air can circulate around them. Do not wash before storing.
4. Wash other fresh vegetables as soon as they come from the market, except those already prepared and bagged. Never soak vegetables in water. Rinse head vegetables (lettuce, cabbage, etc.), under running water but keep heads intact. Do not cut open and do not loosen leaves before storing. Remove all excess moisture after washing vegetables. Store immediately in the crisping pan of the refrigerator or wrap in food bags, waxed paper, or foil before placing in the refrigerator.

BEFORE COOKING

1. Always prepare vegetables as close to cooking time as possible.
2. With a stiff vegetable brush, scrub well.
3. If it is necessary to peel vegetables, use a vegetable peeler and pare skins as thin as possible.
4. Rinse in cold water, if desired, but do not let vegetables stand in water; it can dissolve some precious vitamins and minerals.
5. Follow directions listed for individual vegetables for specific suggestions for cleaning and preparing.

COOKING FRESH VEGETABLES

1. Prepare vegetables according to the directions given under each type. Cut into pieces as specified.
2. Place vegetables in a pan that they most nearly fill.
3. Add 3 ounces water.
4. Put cover on pan with vac-control valve open.
5. Place over medium-high heat.
6. Allow vapor to escape through vac-control valve 3 to 5 minutes.
7. Close vac-control valve and turn off heat. Do not remove cover.
8. Let stand 15 to 20 minutes.

The steaming time given in the general directions allows for freshness of vegetables and sizes into which they are cut. As you become accustomed to this new method of cooking, you will know exactly how long each vegetable must cook to become tender.

If you remove the cover to test the vegetable and it is not tender enough, reheat utensil again over medium-high heat, with vac-control valve open. Steam for one minute. Close vac-control valve and turn off heat. Let stand the remainder of recommended time.

Note: It is possible to have good cooking results even if the utensil is only a third or half full. When cooking in a 4-quart or larger utensil, follow the above procedure with these exceptions: use 4 ounces of water and permit vapor to escape 4 to 5 minutes before turning off heat.

Warning: At altitudes above 2,000 feet, use 4 ounces of water and allow vapor to escape for 5 minutes before turning off heat. Allow the pan to stand for 15 to 20 minutes.

How to Cook Vegetables

Clean all vegetables well. Some winter vegetables with tough skins can be thinly pared or scraped.

Cut up or leave whole. Place vegetables in a pan that they most nearly fill. Add 3 ounces of water.

FROZEN VEGETABLES

Frozen vegetables are available all year long. They are always in season so your selection is unlimited. The best of the crop is harvested at the peak of quality and rapidly frozen within a few hours.

Buy frozen vegetables from a grocer who keeps them in a freezer cabinet that maintains 0° temperature. They should frozen very solid, not beginning to soften. If they are soft, it is wise to avoid them.

Be on the alert for sales in frozen vegetables. They are always a good buy, provided you have the freezer space available.

COOKING FROZEN VEGETABLES

1. Place block of frozen vegetables in a small saucepan. Add 3 ounces water.
2. Cover, with vac-control valve open. Place saucepan over medium high heat.
3. Allow vapor to escape through vac-control valve for 3 to 5 minutes.
4. Close vac-control valve. Do not remove cover. Turn off heat.

5. Let vegetables stand according to times shown in chart below.

Vegetable	Minutes of vapor time	Minutes of standing time
Asparagus, cut	3 to 5	5 to 8
Artichoke Hearts	3 to 5	8 to 10
Green Beans		
Cut	3 to 5	10 to 15
French	3 to 5	8 to 10
Lima Beans	3 to 5	15 to 20
Brussels Sprouts	3 to 5	10 to 15
Broccoli, chopped	3 to 5	10 to 12
Cauliflower	3 to 5	8 to 10
Corn	3 to 5	4 to 5
Peas	3 to 5	10 to 12
Spinach, chopped	3 to 5	5 to 8

CANNED VEGETABLES

These offer a wonderful variety to choose from and often make a pleasing change in pace. To preserve the delicious flavor in canned vegetables, heat as follows. Drain the liquid from canned peas, lima beans, green beans, carrots and similar vegetables that are packed in liquid, into a saucepan. Boil it down to half or one third in volume. Add vegetables and heat gently. Season to taste with

Cover pan with vac-control valve open.
Place over medium-high heat. Let vapor escape
through vac-control valve for 3 to 5 minutes.

Close vac-control valve and turn off heat.
Do not remove cover. Let pan stand for length of
time recommended in recipe.

salt, pepper and butter or margarine.

Tomatoes, cream style corn and squash should be heated just as it comes from the can. Season to taste before serving.

Canned mushrooms will add a different touch to many of your favorite dishes. They come whole, sliced or chopped in their own mushroom broth. A 3 to 4 ounce can of mushrooms equals about ½ pound of fresh mushrooms.

SEASONING

Perfectly cooked vegetables are always good eating when seasoned with butter or margarine and salt and pepper to taste. For a change try adding garlic, onion or celery salt instead of regular salt. Add a pinch of Ac'cent to bring out the flavor. For a change try a seasoned pepper, a pinch of herbs or a dash of Tabasco. There are always new seasonings on the grocery shelves which you may like to try.

Light cream, which has been heated, goes nicely on many vegetables. Some grated cheese mixed in offers another change. Many people also like hot vegetables, seasoned to taste, and sprinkled with grated Parmesan cheese. Canned soups, such as Cheddar cheese, tomato or cream of mushroom offer a quick and easy sauce for many vegetables.

GREAT GO-TOGETHERS:

Green beans with mushrooms, onions, tomatoes or celery
Lima beans with corn, tomatoes, or onions
Brussels sprouts with chestnuts or celery
Cabbage with lima beans, green peppers, or tomatoes
Carrots with peas, onions, or celery
Cauliflower with corn or mushrooms
Celery with peas, beans, parsnips, or mushrooms
Corn with tomatoes, eggplant, or green peppers
Eggplant with tomatoes, green peppers, or mushrooms
Parsnips with tomatoes or celery
Peas with carrots, onions, celery, potatoes, cucumbers, or turnips
Peas with scallions, mushrooms or garlic
Potatoes with peas or onions
Spinach as a ring or nest for almost any vegetable
Spinach with chopped garlic
Squash with tomatoes or corn
Tomatoes with beans, onions, mushrooms, corn, eggplant, parsnips, green peppers, or cabbage
Turnips with peas

Eggplant Moussaka

ARTICHOKES

Buy green, compact, tightly closed heads. As artichokes get older, the heads open out. Watch out for brown leaves.

Place artichoke on its side on a cutting board. Cut about 1 inch off top with a sharp knife; cut off bottom stem about ½ to 1 inch from base. Pull off outside bottom leaves. With a pair of kitchen scissors, snip off thorny tips on leaves.

1. Place artichokes upright in a saucepan just big enough to hold them snugly. For each artichoke add 1 tablespoon salad oil. Add 1 or 2 cloves garlic and 2 slices lemon.
2. Pour in 1 inch water.
3. Put cover on pan with vac-control valve open.
4. Place over medium-high heat.
5. Allow vapor to escape through vac-control valve 5 minutes.
6. Close vac-control valve and turn heat to low.
7. Simmer artichokes 20 to 40 minutes, depending on size. They are done when a leaf can be easily pulled from the stalk, or stem can be easily pierced with a fork.
8. Lift out artichokes with tongs, and drain upside down. Cut off stubs of stems.
9. Place on salad plates and serve with small cups of melted butter with a squeeze of lemon juice.
10. To eat, pluck off leaves, one by one. Dip base (light colored end) into butter. Scrape off pulp at base with teeth and discard remaining leaf. Eat all leaves in this manner, then cut away choke (fuzzy center) with a fork and knife. Discard choke, leaving heart (bottom). Cut heart into chunks and dip into butter to eat.
11. One artichoke makes one serving.

FRIED ARTICHOKES

1 package (9 ounces) frozen artichoke hearts
Salt and pepper
2 eggs
1 cup seasoned bread crumbs
1 tablespoon chopped parsley
¼ cup olive oil

1. Cook artichoke hearts according to directions for cooking frozen vegetables but do not cook the entire length of time. Artichoke hearts should still be slightly underdone. Drain well. Cool. Cut each artichoke heart in half and sprinkle with salt and pepper.
2. Beat eggs with a fork in a small bowl. Combine bread crumbs and parsley. Dip artichoke hearts in eggs and roll in bread crumbs.
3. Heat oil in skillet over medium-high heat. Fry artichoke hearts about 3 minutes on each side or until golden brown.
4. Serve very hot.
5. Makes 3 to 4 servings.

ARTICHOKE HEARTS WITH MUSHROOMS

1 package (9 ounces) frozen artichoke hearts
1 can (4 ounces) sliced mushrooms
1½ teaspoons cornstarch
2 tablespoons dry sherry
2 tablespoons butter
½ teaspoon lemon juice
Salt
Onion salt
Garlic salt
Pepper
1 tablespoon chopped parsley

1. Cook artichoke hearts according to directions for cooking frozen vegetables. Drain.
2. Drain mushrooms, reserving liquid.
3. Mix cornstarch and sherry in a saucepan, stirring until smooth. Stir in mushroom liquid. Cook over medium heat, stirring constantly, until mixture is thickened and clear. Add salt, onion salt, garlic salt, and pepper to taste. Stir in parsley.
3. Add artichoke hearts and mushrooms. Heat gently before serving.
4. Makes 3 to 4 servings.

ASPARAGUS

Buy straight, green, crisp stalks with close, compact heads. Select stalks of uniform size so that they will all cook for the same length of time.

Break off each stalk as far down as it will snap easily. Scrub lightly with a soft brush and remove scales with a knife, or remove scales and thinly pare the stalks with a vegetable peeler. The latter method is recommended if stalks are very thick and tough, and if the asparagus is very sandy.

1. Lay asparagus in one or two layers in large skillet.
2. Add 3 ounces water.
3. Put cover on pan with vac-control valve open.
4. Place over medium-high heat.
5. Allow vapor to escape through vac-control valve 3 minutes.
6. Close vac-control valve and turn off heat. Do not remove cover.
7. Let stand 10 minutes.
8. Season to taste.
9. Two pounds make 4 servings.

ASPARAGUS VINAIGRETTE BUNDLES

6 tablespoons salad oil
3 tablespoons vinegar
⅛ teaspoon Tabasco
½ teaspoon sugar
¼ teaspoon salt
1 small onion, sliced
2 dozen asparagus spears, cooked (fresh, frozen, or canned)
Pimiento strips

1. Combine salad oil, vinegar, Tabasco, sugar, and salt. Beat until blended. Add onion.
2. Place asparagus spears in a shallow dish, Pour sauce over asparagus and let stand in refrigerator several hours or overnight.
3. Place pimiento strips around 4 or 5 asparagus spears. Secure strips with a wooden pick.
4. Serve as a cold vegetable with meat, or place bundles on lettuce cups and serve as a salad.
5. Makes 5 or 6 servings.

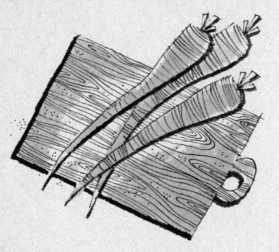

GREEN BEANS

Choose crisp, brightly colored, fully formed pods. To test for freshness, snap a bean between the fingers. If bean is fresh, it will snap; if it is aged, it will merely bend.

Wash beans. Remove ends and cut beans into pieces or leave whole. For whole beans, select beans of uniform size.

1. Place beans in a pan that they most nearly fill.
2. Add 3 ounces water.
3. Put cover on pan with vac-control valve open.
4. Place over medium-high heat.
5. Allow vapor to escape through vac-control valve 3 to 5 minutes.
6. Close vac-control valve and turn off heat. Do not remove cover.
7. Let stand 15 to 20 minutes.
8. Season to taste.
9. One pound makes 3 to 4 servings.

DUTCH GREEN BEANS

1 pound green beans
1 clove garlic, split
1 bay leaf
1 small onion, chopped
2 whole cloves
1 teaspoon vinegar
1 teaspoon sugar
1 tablespoon butter
Salt
Pepper

1. Wash beans. Remove ends from beans and cut in 1-inch pieces on a slant.
2. Cook according to directions given in basic recipe, adding garlic, bay leaf, and onion to beans before cooking.
3. Drain beans, reserving cooking liquid. Discard bay leaf and garlic.
4. Combine cooking liquid, cloves, vinegar, sugar, butter, a dash of salt and a dash of pepper in a small saucepan. Bring to a boil. Remove cloves.
5. Return cooked beans to saucepan and toss lightly. Serve piping hot.
6. Makes 3 to 4 servings.

PEPPERED BEANS

1 pound green beans
2 tablespoons olive oil
½ red or green pepper, slivered
¼ cup blanched slivered almonds
Salt and pepper
1 tablespoon snipped parsley

1. Wash beans. Remove ends and leave whole.
2. Cook according to directions given in basic recipe.
3. Heat olive oil in a small skillet over medium heat. Add green pepper and almonds and cook, stirring occasionally, until pepper is limp and nuts are lightly browned.
4. Combine with hot cooked green beans. Season to taste with salt and pepper.
5. Serve immediately sprinkled with parsley.
6. Makes 3 to 4 servings.

GREEN BEANS AND MUSHROOMS

1 pound green beans
2 teaspoons minced onions
1 can (6 ounces) sliced mushrooms
2 tablespoons butter
Salt and pepper

1. Wash beans. Cut off ends and cut into 1-inch lengths.
2. Place beans in pan, add onion and cook beans as directed in basic recipe.
3. Drain mushrooms. Melt butter in a small skillet. Add mushrooms and cook over low heat until lightly browned.
4. Combine beans and mushrooms. Season to taste with salt and pepper.
5. Makes 4 servings.

GREEN BEANS PIQUANT

1 pound green beans
2 tablespoons butter or margarine
1 teaspoon prepared mustard
1 tablespoon Worcestershire sauce
Salt and pepper

1. Wash beans. Remove ends. Cut into 2-inch pieces.
2. Cook beans according to directions in basic recipe.
3. When beans are tender, add butter, mustard, and Worcestershire sauce. Toss lightly until butter is melted and beans are well coated with mixture. Add salt and a dash of freshly ground pepper to taste.
4. Makes 3 to 4 servings.

HERBED GREEN BEANS

1 pound green beans
2 tablespoons butter
½ cup minced onions
1 clove garlic, minced
2 tablespoons snipped parsley
¼ teaspoon dried rosemary
¼ teaspoon dried basil
¾ teaspoon salt

1. Wash beans. Remove ends and strings, if any. Cut into 2-inch pieces.
2. Cook beans according to directions in basic recipe.
3. Melt butter in a small saucepan. Add onions and garlic and cook gently for 5 minutes, until tender but not browned.
4. Add parsley, rosemary, basil and salt. Cover and simmer gently 5 minutes.
5. Turn green beans into a warmed serving dish. Add herb mixture and toss lightly. Serve immediately.
6. Makes 4 servings.

VIENNESE SNAP BEANS

1½ pounds green beans
1 tablespoon butter
1 tablespoon flour
1 sprig parsley, minced
2 slices onion, minced
½ cup fresh dill, minced
½ teaspoon salt
Dash of pepper
2 tablespoons sour cream
1 teaspoon vinegar

1. Wash green beans. Snap off ends and cut into julienne strips.
2. Cook beans according to directions in basic recipe.
3. Melt butter in a small saucepan over low heat. Add flour, parsley, and onions. Stir over low heat about 2 minutes.
4. Drain liquid from beans into a measuring cup. Add enough water to make ¾ cup bean liquid. Stir liquid into butter-flour mixture. Cook over low heat, stirring constantly, until smooth and slightly thickened.
5. Add dill and simmer 5 minutes.
6. Add beans, salt, pepper, sour cream, and vinegar. Heat thoroughly but do not boil.
7. Makes 6 servings.

SAVORY GREEN BEANS

1 pound green beans
2 tablespoons olive oil
1 small clove garlic, minced
1 teaspoon catsup
1 teaspoon Worcestershire sauce
¼ teaspoon savory
Salt

1. Wash beans. Remove ends and cut beans in half.
2. Cook beans according to directions in basic recipe.
3. While beans are cooking, heat olive oil in small saucepan over medium heat. Add garlic and cook slowly, stirring constantly, until garlic is tender but not browned. Stir in catsup, Worcestershire sauce and savory.
4. Toss cooked beans with garlic sauce. Season to taste with salt. Serve piping hot.
5. Makes 3 to 4 servings.

GREEN BEANS ITALIANO

1 pound green beans
1 medium-sized onion, thinly sliced
⅓ cup catsup
¼ teaspoon oregano
Salt to taste

1. Wash and remove ends from beans. Cut into ½-inch lengths. Place in saucepan that is most nearly filled by beans. Place onions on top of beans.
2. Cook beans and onions according to directions in basic recipe.
3. Combine catsup and oregano. When beans are tender, stir in catsup mixture and serve immediately.
4. Makes 4 servings.

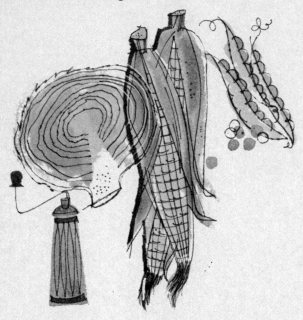

BEETS

Spring beets are small, well shaped red root vegetables. Select by freshness of the top greens. Beet tops can be removed and cooked on day of purchase in same manner as spinach. Beets will keep several days in the refrigerator.

Cut tops off beets, and peel, if necessary, very thinly. Cut beets into slices or small cubes. Mature beets are apt to be woody in texture and will take longer to cook than younger beets.

1. Place beets in a pan that they most nearly fill.
2. Add 3 ounces water.
3. Put cover on pan with vac-control valve open.
4. Place over medium high heat.
5. Allow vapor to escape through vac-control valve 3 to 5 minutes.
6. Close vac-control valve and turn off heat. Do not remove cover.
7. Let stand 20 minutes.
8. Season to taste.
9. 1 to 1½ pounds beets make 4 servings.

BEETS WITH CLARET SAUCE

1½ pounds beets
2 tablespoons butter
1 tablespoon flour
1 teaspoon sugar
Dash of nutmeg
Salt and pepper
¼ cup liquid from cooked beets
¼ cup claret

1. Wash beets and peel if necessary. Cut beets into julienne strips.
2. Cook according to directions in basic recipe.
3. Melt butter in a small saucepan. Blend in flour and seasonings. Remove from heat.
4. Drain liquid from cooked beets into a measuring cup. Add enough water to make ¼ cup liquid. Stir into butter-flour mixture.
5. Cook over low heat, stirring constantly, until smooth and thickened. Stir in claret.
6. Add beets and cook over very low heat until beets are well coated and heated through.
7. Makes 4 servings.

BEETS IN ORANGE SAUCE

2 bunches medium-sized beets
1 tablespoon cornstarch
¾ teaspoon salt
1½ tablespoons sugar
¼ cup orange juice
Reserved beet liquid
2 tablespoons lemon juice
½ teaspoon grated orange rind
1 tablespoon butter or margarine

1. Scrub beets. Cut off tops. Peel if necessary and cut into small cubes.
2. Cook beets according to directions in basic recipe.
3. When beets are cooked, measure remaining liquid into a measuring cup. Add sufficient water to make ½ cup beet liquid.
4. Combine cornstarch, salt, sugar, orange juice and reserved beet juice in a saucepan.
5. Cook over medium heat, stirring constantly, until thick and smooth.
6. Add lemon juice, orange rind, and butter.
7. Add beets and heat thoroughly over medium heat.
8. Makes 4 servings.

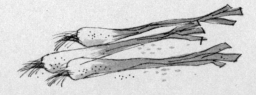

HARVARD BEETS

⅓ cup sugar
½ teaspoon salt
1 tablespoon cornstarch
½ cup vinegar
2 tablespoons butter or margarine
1 teaspoon minced onion
3 cups hot sliced cooked or canned beets (if fresh beets not available), drained

1. Combine sugar, salt and cornstarch in top part of double boiler. Stir in vinegar and cook over low heat, stirring constantly, until smooth and thickened.
2. Add butter, onion and beets. Place over hot water and cook 15 to 20 minutes.
3. Makes 5 servings.

BROCCOLI

Choose broccoli that is a bright, dark green color with compact buds and small leaves. Avoid woody or limp stalks.

Cut off tough bottom ends of stalks and remove large leaves. Wash thoroughly. If stalks are large, remove tough outer skin with vegetable peeler. Cut very large stalks in halves or quarters. Make crosswise slits in stalks lengthwise, almost up to flowerets.

1. Place broccoli in a pan that it most nearly fills.
2. Add 3 ounces water.
3. Put cover on pan with vac-control valve open.
4. Place over medium high heat.
5. Allow vapor to escape through vac-control valve 3 to 5 minutes.
6. Close vac-control valve and turn off heat. Do not remove cover.
7. Let stand 18 to 20 minutes.
8. Season to taste.
9. 1 bunch makes 3 to 4 servings.

BROCCOLI INDIENNE

1 bunch broccoli
⅓ cup chicken bouillon
1 bay leaf
¼ teaspoon thyme
2 tablespoons lemon juice
1 tablespoon butter
Salt

1. Wash broccoli. Cut off tough bottom stalks and discard. Remove leaves. Cut stems into chunks and leave flowerets intact.
2. Place stem chunks in bottom of saucepan and flowerets on top of stems. Add chicken bouillon, bay leaf and thyme.
3. Cook according to directions in basic recipe.
4. Discard bay leaf. Add lemon juice and butter. Toss very lightly and season to taste with salt.
5. Makes 3 to 4 servings.

BROCCOLI WITH SOUR CREAM SAUCE

1 bunch fresh broccoli
2 tablespoons butter
2 tablespoons minced onion
2 teaspoons sugar
1 teaspoon vinegar
⅛ teaspoon pepper
1½ cups dairy sour cream

1. Prepare and cook broccoli according to directions given in basic recipe.
2. While broccoli is cooking, melt butter in top of a double boiler over medium heat. Add onion and cook until onion is tender, but not browned.
3. Remove from heat and stir in sugar, vinegar and pepper. Gently blend in sour cream. Place top of double boiler over warm, not boiling, water. Heat until sauce is warm.
4. Serve sauce over cooked broccoli.
5. Makes 4 servings.

BRUSSELS SPROUTS

Brussels sprouts look like miniature cabbage heads. Select firm, solid, round heads of bright green color. Avoid yellow spots or worm holes.

Remove imperfect leaves and cut off bit of stem end. Rinse thoroughly.

1. Place brussels sprouts in a pan that they most nearly fill.
2. Add 3 ounces water.
3. Put cover on pan with vac-control valve open.
4. Place over medium-high heat.
5. Allow vapor to escape through vac-control valve 3 to 5 minutes.
6. Close vac-control valve and turn off heat. Do not remove cover.
7. Let stand 15 to 20 minutes.
8. Season to taste.
9. 1 pound makes 4 servings.

CARAWAY BRUSSELS SPROUTS

1 pound brussels sprouts
Grated rind of 1 lemon
1 tablespoon lemon juice
1 tablespoon butter
1 teaspoon caraway seeds
½ cup dairy sour cream

1. Remove imperfect leaves and cut off bit of stem end. Rinse thoroughly in cold water.
2. Cook according to directions given in basic recipe. Drain.
3. Add remaining ingredients and heat thoroughly but *do not boil*.
4. Makes 4 servings.

GOLDEN NUGGET BRUSSELS SPROUTS

1 pound brussels sprouts
3 tablespoons butter or margarine
1 tablespoon flour
¼ teaspoon salt
½ cup milk
1 egg yolk
1 teaspoon grated orange peel
¼ cup orange juice
2 tablespoons lemon juice
2 navel oranges, peeled, cut into bite-sized
   pieces

1. Wash brussels sprouts and peel off outer leaves, if needed.
2. Cook brussels sprouts according to directions in basic recipe.
3. While brussels sprouts are cooking, melt 1 tablespoon of the butter in a small saucepan. Stir in flour and salt. Stir in milk and cook over low heat, stirring constantly, until mixture comes to a boil and is thickened.
4. Remove from heat and blend in egg yolk and remaining butter. Stir in grated orange peel, orange juice, and lemon juice.
5. Drain brussels sprouts and combine with drained orange pieces. Add hot sauce and toss lightly.
6. Makes 4 servings.

CABBAGE

Select a fresh-leafed head which is heavy for its size. New cabbage should be very green in color, though rather loose leafed. Mature heads are paler in color and very solid. Savoy or curly cabbage is loose centered with crinkled green leaves. Red cabbage makes a pleasant change and is selected and cooked the same as green cabbage.

Remove outer leaves and wash whole head under running water. Cabbage can be cooked in quarters or shredded. To shred cabbage, cut into quarters. Remove most of core. With a very sharp knife, thinly slice each quarter into medium shreds.

1. Place shredded cabbage in a pan that it most nearly fills.
2. Add 3 ounces water.
3. Put cover on pan with vac-control valve open.
4. Place over medium high heat.
5. Allow vapor to escape through vac-control valve 3 to 5 minutes.
6. Close vac-control valve and turn off heat. Do not remove cover.
7. Let stand 8 to 10 minutes.
8. Season to taste.
9. 1-pound cabbage makes 4 servings.

DUTCH CABBAGE

1 medium-sized cabbage
2 beaten eggs
1 tablespoon melted butter
½ teaspoon salt
   Dash of pepper
¼ cup heavy cream

1. Remove tough outer leaves from cabbage. Shred cabbage.
2. Cook cabbage according to directions in basic recipe.
3. Heat oven to 375°F.
4. Combine remaining ingredients and blend well.
5. Drain cabbage and toss lightly with egg mixture. Turn into a lightly buttered casserole.
6. Bake about 20 minutes or until lightly browned.
7. Makes 6 servings.

NORWEGIAN CABBAGE

1 medium-sized cabbage
½ cup sour cream
½ teaspoon caraway seeds
   Salt and pepper

1. Remove tough outer leaves from cabbage. Shred cabbage.
2. Cook cabbage according to directions in basic recipe.
3. Drain cabbage and toss lightly with sour cream and caraway seeds. Season to taste with salt and pepper. Heat thoroughly over low heat, but *do not boil*.
4. Makes 4 to 6 servings.

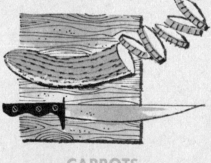

CARROTS

Carrots should be crisp, bright orange with fresh green tops; however, today most carrots come topped and bagged. If they have tops, remove tops and store carrots in the refrigerator.

Scrub carrots thoroughly with a stiff brush. Very tiny fresh spring carrots may be left whole. Cut larger carrots into strips, rings or cubes. If carrots are mature they can be scraped or peeled very thinly before cooking.

1. Place carrots in a pan that they most nearly fill.
2. Add 3 ounces water.
3. Put cover on pan with vac-control valve open.
4. Place over medium-high heat.
5. Allow vapor to escape through vac-control valve 3 to 5 minutes.
6. Close vac-control valve and turn off heat. Do not remove cover.
7. Let sliced carrots stand 15 to 20 minutes. Whole carrots should stand about 25 minutes.
8. Season to taste.
9. 1 pound carrots makes 4 servings.

GLAZED CARROTS

24 small spring carrots
½ cup brown sugar, firmly packed
¼ cup butter
¼ cup hot water

1. Scrub carrots. If they are young spring carrots do not peel. Leave carrots whole.
2. Cook carrots according to directions in basic recipe.
3. Heat oven to 375°F.
4. Combine brown sugar, butter, and water in a small saucepan. Bring to a boil and simmer 5 minutes.
5. Drain carrots and palce in a single layer in a flat baking dish.
6. Brush carrots with syrup and bake 20 minutes, basting occasionally with remaining syrup.
7. Makes 6 servings.

PAN-GLAZED CARROTS

1 pound carrots
½ teaspoon salt
¼ cup butter
4 teaspoons sugar
4 teaspoons chopped chives

1. Scrub carrots. Peel if necessary. Cut into 1½-inch slices.
2. Cook according to directions given in basic recipe, adding salt during cooking time.
3. In a large skillet melt butter and heat until lightly browned. Stir in sugar.
4. Drain carrots. Add carrots to melted butter and heat over medium-low heat, shaking skillet to glaze carrots.
5. Serve sprinkled with chopped chives.
6. Makes 4 servings.

PARSLEY CARROTS

12 medium-sized fresh carrots
3 tablespoons butter or margarine
⅓ cup chopped fresh parsley
¼ teaspoon ground black pepper

1. Scrub carrots. If they are spring carrots do not peel; if they are winter carrots, peel thinly.
2. Cut carrots in rings.
3. Cook according to directions in basic recipe.
4. Melt butter or margarine in a saucepan.
5. Add parsley and pepper. Heat thoroughly.
6. Place cooked carrots in a serving dish. Pour parsley mixture over top. Serve immediately.
7. Makes 6 servings.

CRANBERRY CARROTS

10 medium-sized carrots
1 teaspoon salt
¼ cup butter or margarine
¼ cup canned jellied cranberry sauce
⅛ teaspoon pepper

1. Wash and scrape carrots.
2. Cut diagonally into 1-inch pieces.
3. Cook carrots according to directions in basic recipe, using ½ teaspoon of the salt.
4. Drain carrots.
5. Melt butter in a large skillet.
6. Add cranberry sauce. Cook gently, stirring constantly, until sauce is dissolved.
7. Add carrots, pepper, remaining ½ teaspoon salt.
8. Simmer for 3 to 5 minutes, stirring occasionally.
9. Makes 4 servings.

TANGY GLAZED CARROTS

1 bunch carrots
⅓ cup orange juice
2 tablespoons sugar
¼ teaspoon ground cloves
¼ teaspoon salt
½ jar (5 ounces) pineapple cheese spread

1. Scrub carrots and peel if necessary. Slice carrots into rings. Place in a saucepan that they most nearly fill.
2. Cook carrots according to directions in basic recipe.
3. Combine orange juice, sugar, cloves, salt, and cheese spread. Pour over carrots in saucepan.
4. Place over low heat and simmer, stirring lightly, until cheese melts and mixture is hot. *Do not boil.*
5. Makes 4 servings.

CAULIFLOWER

Choose a head with fresh green outer leaves and a firm, compact, crisp white head. The flower clusters should not have begun to grow. Avoid spotted or bruised heads.

Remove outer leaves and stalks. Separate into flowerets or leave whole.

FLOWERETS

1. Place flowerets in a pan that they most nearly fill.
2. Add 3 ounces water.
3. Put cover on pan with vac-control valve open.
4. Place over medium high heat.
5. Allow vapor to escape through vac-control valve 3 to 5 minutes.
6. Close vac-control valve and turn off heat. Do not remove cover.
7. Let stand 15 to 20 minutes.
8. Season to taste.
9. 1 large head cauliflower makes 4 servings.

WHOLE

1. Place whole head of cauliflower in a deep saucepan.
2. Add 3 ounces water.
3. Put cover on pan with vac-control valve open.
4. Place over medium high heat.
5. Allow vapor to escape through vac-control valve 3 to 5 minutes.
6. Close vac-control valve and turn off heat. Do not remove cover.
7. Let stand 20 minutes.
8. Season to taste.
9. 1 large head cauliflower makes 4 servings.

CAULIFLOWER AND TOMATOES

1 head cauliflower
1 small clove garlic
3 tablespoons olive oil
½ teaspoon salt
½ cup cooked tomatoes
1 teaspoon chopped parsley
2 tablespoons grated Parmesan cheese

1. Remove outer leaves and stalks from cauliflower. Separate into flowerets.
2. Cook according to directions in basic recipe, but undercook just slightly.
3. Sauté garlic in hot olive oil until lightly browned. Remove garlic.
4. Drain cauliflower. Add flowerets to hot olive oil and sauté lightly.
5. Add salt and tomatoes. Cover, turn heat to low, and simmer 2 to 3 minutes.
6. Arrange in a serving dish and sprinkle parsley and grated cheese over the top.
7. Makes 4 servings.

CHEESED CAULIFLOWER

1 head cauliflower
3 tablespoons olive oil
1 large onion, thinly sliced
¼ teaspoon salt
   Dash of pepper
¼ cup fine dry bread crumbs
¼ cup grated cheddar cheese

1. Remove outer leaves and stalks from cauliflower. Separate into flowerets.
2. Cook according to directions in basic recipe.
3. Heat olive oil in skillet over medium heat. Add sliced onion and cook, stirring occasionally, until onion is tender and lightly browned. Add salt, pepper and crumbs. Remove from heat.
4. Place cooked cauliflower in a shallow, buttered baking dish. Top with hot onion mixture. Sprinkle with grated cheddar cheese.
5. Place on rack about 4 inches from broiler and broil until cheese melts and browns lightly on top.
6. Makes 4 servings.

CELERY

Stalks should be crisp and topped with fresh green leaves. There are two types of celery: Pascal is green, meaty and full-hearted celery with a mild, nutty flavor; golden celery is bleached, white looking and much milder in flavor.

Remove leaves and trim roots. Separate into stalks and scrub, using a brush to remove sand. With a knife, scrape off any discoloration. Use outer branches for cooking. Reserve inner branches to serve raw. Use leaves as flavoring in vegetable soups. Celery may be sliced in half moons, diced, or cut into long thin fingers.

1. Place cut-up celery in a pan that it most nearly fills.
2. Add 3 ounces water.
3. Put cover on pan with vac-control valve open.
4. Place over medium high heat.
5. Allow vapor to escape through vac-control valve 3 to 5 minutes.
6. Close vac-control valve and turn off heat. Do not remove cover.
7. Let stand 10 minutes.
8. Season to taste.
9. Allow ½ to ¾ cup diced celery for each serving.

BRAISED CELERY

Celery stalks
3 tablespoons butter
¾ cup water
1 chicken bouillon cube

1. Scrub celery stalks with a stiff brush. Scrape off any discoloration with a knife. Cut stalks into 4-inch lengths. If celery stalks are wide, cut in half lengthwise. Prepare about 36 lengths.
2. Melt butter in skillet. Add celery and cook over medium heat, stirring occasionally, until celery is delicately browned and somewhat tender.
3. Add water and bouillon cube and simmer until celery is tender and liquid reduced to about ¼ cup.
4. Makes about 6 servings.

SWEET AND SOUR CELERY

2 cups thinly sliced celery
½ teaspoon salt
1 bay leaf
3 whole cloves
2 tablespoons sugar
3 tablespoons vinegar
2 tablespoons butter or margarine

1. Place celery in saucepan with salt, bay leaf, cloves and 3 ounces water.
2. Cook according to directions given in basic recipe.
3. When celery is tender remove bay leaf and whole cloves.
4. Add remaining ingredients and heat over low heat, stirring occasionally, until butter is melted and celery is piping hot.
5. Makes 3 to 4 servings.

CORN

Cobs should be well filled with plump kernels that spurt milk when pressed. Husks should be fresh and green, not dried out on top.

Just before cooking remove husks, all silk, and any blemishes or discoloration.

1. Line skillet or Dutch oven with inner husks.
2. Lay ears of corn in skillet or Dutch oven.
3. Add 3 ounces water.
4. Put cover on pan with vac-control valve open.
5. Allow vapor to escape through vac-control valve 3 to 5 minutes.
6. Close vac-control valve and turn off heat. Do not remove cover.
   Do not remove cover.
8. Let stand 10 minutes.
9. Serve with butter and salt.
10. Allow 1 or 2 ears of corn for each serving.

Note: To serve off the cob: With a very sharp knife, slice kernels from hot, cooked corn, being careful not to cut too close to the cob.

CORN PUDDING

2 cups chopped cooked or canned whole kernel corn
2 eggs, slightly beaten
1 teaspoon sugar
1½ tablespoons melted butter or margarine
2 cups milk, heated
1¾ teaspoon salt
¼ teaspoon pepper

1. Heat oven to 325°F.
2. Combine all ingredients and blend well. Pour into a 1½-quart buttered casserole. Set casserole in a pan of hot water.
3. Bake 1 hour and 15 minutes.
4. Makes 6 servings.

MEXICAN CORN

1 (No. 2) can whole-kernel corn
2 tablespoons butter
1 tablespoon chopped pimiento
1 tablespoon chopped green pepper
½ teaspoon salt
1 teaspoon chili powder

1. Turn corn into a saucepan.
2. Add remaining ingredients and simmer 10 to 15 minutes, stirring frequently. Serve piping hot.
3. Makes 4 servings.

EGGPLANT

Choose firm, heavy eggplant with a rich purple color and a shiny smooth skin with no rust spots. Wash and pare if necessary when ready to use. Do not soak in salt or salt water before cooking.

1. Peel eggplant if the skin is very tough.
2. Cut into slices ¼-inch thick.
3. Sprinkle with salt, pepper, and a little flour.
4. Heat a small amount of oil in the large skillet over medium heat.
5. Fry eggplant in hot oil until golden brown on both sides, about 6 to 8 minutes.
6. Drain on absorbent paper. Serve immediately.
7. 1 medium-sized egg plant, about 1½ pounds, makes 4 servings.

EGGPLANT MOUSSAKA

1 large eggplant
Oil for frying
4 medium onions, sliced
1 clove garlic, minced
½ pound ground lamb
2 cans (8 ounces each) tomato sauce
1 teaspoon salt
1 teaspoon oregano
2 tablespoons butter
2 tablespoons flour
½ teaspoon salt
⅛ teaspoon nutmeg
1½ cups milk
2 egg yolks, beaten

1. Slice eggplant, without peeling, into ¼ - to ½ -inch thick slices.
2. Heat oil in skillet over medium-high heat. Sauté egg plant slices until lightly browned on both sides. Drain on paper toweling.
3. Place onions, garlic and lamb in a clean skillet. Cook over medium-high heat, stirring occasionally, until lamb is lightly browned and onions are limp. Drain off as much accumulated fat as possible.
4. Add tomato sauce, salt and oregano. Cover with vac-control valve closed. Lower heat and simmer about 20 minutes, or just long enough to blend flavors.
5. Melt the butter in a small saucepan over medium heat. Stir in flour, salt and nutmeg. Remove from heat and add milk. Cook over medium heat, stirring constantly, until mixture is smooth and thick. Stir a small amount of the hot mixture into beaten egg yolks. Return to mixture in pan and stir well. Cook for 1 minute, stirring constantly. Remove from heat.
6. Heat oven to 350°F.
7. Place a layer of egg plant on the bottom of a 2-quart casserole. Top with a layer of lamb-tomato mixture. Repeat process until egg plant and lamb mixture are used. Pour cream sauce over the top.
8. Bake 1 hour or until mixture is very hot and bubbly.
9. Makes 4 to 6 servings.

LIMA BEANS

Select pods that are well filled, crisp, fresh, and dark green in color. The shelled beans should be plump and have a tender skin which is green or greenish-white in color.

Wash pods and then shell beans just before cooking. For ease in shelling, cut off thin outer edge of pod with a sharp knife or scissors, then slip out the beans.

1. Place beans in a pan that they most nearly fill.
2. Add 3 ounces water.
3. Put cover on pan with vac-control valve open.
4. Place over medium high heat.
5. Allow vapor to escape through vac-control valve 3 to 5 minutes.
6. Close vac-contro valve and turn off heat. Do not remove cover.
7. Let stand 20 minutes.
8. Season to taste.
9. 2 to 3 pounds make 4 servings.

LIMA BEANS PARMESAN

2½ pounds lima beans
¼ cup chicken bouillon
1 bay leaf
1 clove garlic
4 strips bacon
Salt and pepper
Grated Parmesan cheese

1. Shell lima beans.
2. Place in a saucepan with chicken bouillon, bay leaf and garlic. Cook according to directions given in basic recipe.
3. Pan fry bacon over medium heat until crisp. Drain on paper towels.
4. Season beans to taste with salt and pepper. Crumble bacon and toss with beans.
5. Serve with Parmesan cheese sprinkled on top of beans.
6. Makes 4 servings.

LIMAS PIMIENTO

2 pounds fresh lima beans
1½ teaspoons salt
2 canned pimientos
2 tablespoons butter or margarine
½ teaspoon onion salt
⅛ teaspoon pepper

1. Shell lima beans.
2. Cook lima beans according to directions in basic recipe, using 1 teaspoon salt.
3. Cut pimientos into small pieces.
4. Drain beans well.
5. Add butter, remaining ½ teaspoon salt, onion salt, pepper, and chopped pimiento to drained beans.
6. Heat thoroughly.
7. Makes 4 servings.

MUSHROOMS

Buy firm, clean, moist, and plump white to creamy white mushrooms with short stems. Mushrooms should be free of spots and not wrinkled.

Wash quickly, if necessary. Do not peel. Leave whole for a vegetable. Remove stems and stuff caps for an appetizer or vegetable. Chop mushrooms to use with other vegetables or meat dishes.

BROILED MUSHROOMS

1 dozen large mushroom caps
Melted butter
Salt and pepper

1. Place cleaned mushrooms, rounded sides down, on a broiler pan. Brush with melted butter and sprinkle with a little salt and pepper.
2. Place broiler pan about 4 inches from source of heat and broil 7 to 9 minutes.
3. Makes 4 servings.

ITALIAN STYLE MUSHROOMS

1 pound mushrooms
3 tablespoons olive oil
1 clove garlic
½ teaspoon salt
¼ teaspoon pepper
1 tablespoon butter
2 tablespoons chopped parsley
Juice of half a lemon

1. Wash mushrooms, if needed. Slice thinly.
2. Heat olive oil in skillet and brown garlic in hot oil. Remove garlic.

3. Add mushrooms, salt and pepper. Cook over medium-high heat, stirring occasionally, until liquid evaporates.
4. Add butter and parsley and cook over medium heat 5 minutes.
5. Remove from heat, add lemon juice and serve immediately.
6. Makes 4 servings.

STUFFED MUSHROOMS

12 large mushrooms
1 tablespoon chopped parsley
2 tablespoons minced onion
2 tablespoons butter
1 tablespoon fine bread crumbs
¼ teaspoon salt
2⅛ teaspoon mace
2 egg yolks, slightly beaten

1. Heat oven to 400°F.
2. Wash mushrooms if needed and drain well. Remove stems and chop fine.
3. Combine stems, parsley, onion, and butter in a small skillet. Cook over low heat, stirring, for 5 minutes.
4. Stir in crumbs, salt, and mace. Remove from heat. Stir in egg yolks.
5. Pile mixture lightly into inverted mushroom caps.
6. Place in a shallow buttered baking pan. Bake 15 minutes or until well browned.
7. Makes 4 to 6 servings.

ONIONS

Dry onions should be bright, clean, hard and well shaped with dry skins. Do not buy onions that are damp, or that have developed stems or shoots. Yellow onions, chopped, minced and sliced, add immeasurably to main dishes. They are excellent french fried or pan fried as an accompaniment to other foods. Small white dry onions are excellent as a whole cooked vegetable.

To avoid weeping when peeling white onions, pour boiling water over onions, then rinse in cold water. Cut off a slice from stem and root ends and slip off skins.

1. Place peeled white onions in a pan that they most nearly fill.
2. Add 3 ounces water.
3. Place cover on pan with vac-control valve open.
4. Place over medium-high heat.
5. Allow vapor to escape through vac-control valve 5 minutes.
6. Close vac-control valve and turn off heat. Do not remove cover.
7. Let stand 18 to 22 minutes.
8. Season to taste.
9. 1½ pounds onions makes 4 servings.

CREAMED ONIONS AND PEAS SAUTERNE

2 pounds small white onions
1 package (12 ounces) frozen peas
¼ cup butter or margarine
¼ cup flour
1 cup light cream
⅓ cup sauterne or white table wine
2 tablespoons minced parsley
    Salt and pepper to taste

1. Heat oven to 400°F.
2. Peel onions. Cook according to directions in basic recipe.
3. Drain liquid from onions into a measuring cup. Add enough cold water to make ½ cup liquid.
4. Cook peas according to directions; drain.
5. Melt butter in a small saucepan. Stir in flour. Remove from heat and stir in cream, reserved liquid from onions, and sauterne.
6. Cook over medium heat, stirring constantly, until mixture thickens and comes to a boil.
7. Remove from heat and add parsley, salt, and pepper.
8. Combine sauce with onions and peas. Turn into a buttered casserole.
9. Bake for 20 minutes.
10. Makes about 8 servings.

* * * * * *

SUNNY BAKED ONIONS

6 medium yellow onions
2 teaspoons grated orange peel
3 tablespoons brown sugar
2 navel oranges, peeled and cut into ½-inch slices, crosswise
2 tablespoons butter or margarine
    Nutmeg
1 cup orange juice
½ teaspoon salt
½ cup sliced, toasted almonds

1. Heat oven to 400°F.
2. Carefully peel onions and cut a thin slice off top and bottom of each onion.
3. Place in a casserole, cut side up. Sprinkle tops with grated orange peel and brown sugar. Top each onion with an orange slice. Dot with butter and sprinkle lightly with nutmeg. Add orange juice and salt.
4. Cover casserole and bake 1 to 1¼ hours, or until just tender, but not mushy.
5. Serve hot, garnished with toasted almonds and orange sauce from casserole.
6. Makes 6 servings.

GREEN ONIONS

Green onions are marketed in bunches. Buy onions with crisp, green tops and medium-sized, well formed heads that are blanched 2 to 3 inches from the root. Green onions are usually eaten raw, in salads, or cooked with other vegetables as flavoring. However they make a different cooked vegetable served hot or cold.

Wash onions well, cut off roots and remove any loose skin. Cut about 4 inches off the green tops and discard.

1. Lay onions flat in a pan that they most nearly fill.
2. Add 3 ounces water.
3. Put cover on pan with vac-control valve open.
4. Place over medium-high heat.
5. Allow vapor to escape through vac-control valve 3 to 5 minutes.
6. Close vac-control valve and turn off heat. Do not remove cover.
7. Let stand 10 to 15 minutes.
8. Season with salt, pepper and a little melted butter.
9. 2 bunches makes about 4 servings.

Note: To serve chilled as an appetizer or vegetable do not add melted butter. When onions are cold, cover with French dressing and chill about 2 hours before serving.

PEAS

Buy bright green, fresh looking pods, somewhat velvety to the touch.

Just before serving, shell by pressing pods between thumb and forefinger to open; then remove peas. Discard any peas that have shoots. Reserve a few pods to cook with peas.

1. Place peas in a pan that they most nearly fill. Add a few pea pods for flavor.
2. Add 3 ounces water.
3. Put cover on pan with vac-control valve open.
4. Place over medium-high heat.
5. Allow vapor to escape through vac-control valve 3 to 5 minutes.
6. Close vac-control valve and turn off heat. Do not remove cover.
7. Let stand 10-15 minutes.
8. Season to taste.
9. 3 pounds fresh peas makes 4 servings.

CREAMED PEAS AND MUSHROOMS

3 pounds peas
¼ pound fresh mushrooms, sliced
¼ teaspoon grated onion
3 tablespoons butter
2 tablespoons flour
1 cup milk
½ teaspoon salt
Dash of pepper
Dash of nutmeg

1. Shell peas. Cook according to directions in basic recipe.
2. Cook mushrooms and onion in hot butter in a saucepan, over medium heat, until mushrooms are tender but not browned.
3. Remove from heat and stir in flour. Gradually stir in milk.
4. Cook over medium heat, stirring constantly, until sauce is smooth and thickened. Add salt, pepper, and nutmeg.
5. Drain peas and stir lightly into sauce. Add more salt if needed.
6. Makes 4 servings.

PEAS PARISIENNE

2 tablespoons butter or margarine
1 cup sliced mushrooms
¼ cup minced onion
¼ teaspoon salt
Dash of pepper
¼ teaspoon nutmeg
⅛ teaspoon dried marjoram
2 tablespoons sherry
2 cups drained cooked peas

1. Melt butter in a skillet. Add mushrooms and onion and cook over medium heat, stirring constantly, until onion is tender, about 5 minutes.
2. Add remaining ingredients and heat thoroughly. Serve immediately.
3. Makes 4 servings.

POTATOES

Buy uniform, well shaped potatoes. Avoid those that have sprouted. Use baking potatoes for baking and for frying. Use new potatoes cooked and in salads.

Scrub thoroughly with a stiff brush. Remove blemishes and eyes with a sharp knife. To save food value cook with skins on. If necessary, scrape or pare with a vegetable peeler. Cut potatoes into uniform-size pieces. New potatoes are best scrubbed and cooked whole, or cut in pieces if large.

COOKED POTATOES

1. Place potatoes in a pan that they most nearly fill.
2. Add 3 ounces water.
3. Put cover on pan with vac-control valve open.
4. Place over medium-high heat.
5. Allow vapor to escape through vac-control valve 3 to 5 minutes.
6. Close vac-control valve and turn off heat. Do not remove cover.
7. Let stand 20 minutes.
8. Serve potatoes with butter, salt and pepper. For mashed potatoes, remove skins by putting a few pieces at a time through food press. Whip in hot milk, butter, salt, and pepper.
9. 1½ to 2 pounds makes 4 servings.

BAKED POTATOES

1. Scrub potatoes with a stiff brush. Remove any blemishes.
2. Dry potatoes thoroughly with paper towels. Let stand on dry paper toweling for about 15 minutes so that skins will dry out thoroughly.
3. Pack potatoes tightly together on the bottom of a saucepan.
4. Cover with vac-control valve closed.
5. Place over medium heat until cover is hot to the touch.
6. Do not remove cover at any time during the baking period.
7. Turn heat to low and let stand 45 minutes to 1 hour, depending on size of the potatoes.

CHEDDAR SCALLOPED POTATOES

1 can (10¾ ounces) condensed cheddar cheese soup
½ to ¾ cup milk
Dash pepper
4 cups thinly sliced peeled potatoes
1 small onion, thinly sliced
1 tablespoon butter or margarine
Dash paprika

1. Heat oven to 375°F.
2. Blend together soup, milk, and pepper.
3. In a buttered 1½-quart casserole arrange alternate layers of potatoes, onion, and cheese soup sauce.
4. Dot top with butter. Sprinkle with paprika.
5. Cover casserole and bake 1 hour. Uncover and bake 15 minutes.
6. Makes 4 to 6 servings.

SUMMER SQUASH WITH SOUR CREAM

2½ pounds summer squash
¼ cup butter or margarine
½ cup sliced onion
1¼ teaspoons salt
⅛ teaspoon pepper
1 tablespoon snipped fresh dill
1 cup dairy sour cream

1. Wash squash. Cut on the diagonal into ½-inch slices.
2. Melt butter in large skillet over medium heat. Add onion and cook about 3 minutes.
3. Add squash, salt, pepper, and snipped dill. Toss lightly to combine. Add 3 ounces water.
4. Place cover on skillet with vac-control valve open.
5. Place over medium-high heat.
6. Allow vapor to escape through vac-control valve 3 to 5 minutes.
7. Close vac-control valve and turn off heat. Do not remove cover.
8. Let stand 10 to 12 minutes.
9. Drain squash, if necessary. Turn into serving dish. Spoon sour cream over squash. Serve immediately.
10. Makes 6 servings.

FRIED ZUCCHINI

1½ pound small zucchini
¼ cup butter
1 clove garlic

1. Scrub zucchini and cut in thin slices.
2. Melt butter in skillet. Add garlic and zucchini and cook over medium-low heat, stirring occasionally, about 10 minutes.
3. Cover tightly. Lower heat to very low and simmer 5 minutes, stirring occasionally, until zucchini is tender.
4. Makes 4 to 6 servings.

SWEET POTATOES OR YAMS

Sweet potatoes have yellowish, fawn colored skins and are mealy when cooked. Yams are really sweet potatoes with white to reddish skins, are moist when cooked and have insides that are more orange in color. Buy smooth skinned potatoes with a bright, fresh appearance. Avoid potatoes with dried-out ends. Buy in small amounts, just enough for 1 or 2 meals, as they are perishable.

Scrub potatoes with a stiff brush. Cut potatoes into chunks.

1. Place potatoes in a pan that they most nearly fill.
2. Add 3 ounces water.
3. Put cover on pan with vac-control valve open.
4. Place pan over medium-high heat.
5. Allow vapor to escape through vac-control valve 3 to 5 minutes.
6. Close vac-control valve and turn off heat. Do not remove cover.
7. Let stand 20 to 25 minutes.
8. Serve in their skins with butter, salt and pepper. For mashed potatoes, remove skins by putting a few pieces at a time through food press.
9. 1½ to 2 pounds makes 4 servings.

CANDIED SWEET POTATOES

6 medium-sized sweet potatoes
⅓ cup water
1 cup brown sugar, firmly packed
2 tablespoons butter

1. Heat oven to 400°F.
2. Cook sweet potatoes according to directions in basic recipe.
3. Combine water, sugar, and butter and bring to a boil.
4. Peel sweet potatoes and cut in slices. Place in a buttered baking dish. Pour syrup over the top.
5. Bake 20 minutes, basting with syrup occasionally.
6. Makes 6 servings.

YAMS BAKED IN MARMALADE-WINE SAUCE

2½ pounds yams
1 cup brown sugar, firmly packed
⅓ cup orange marmalade
¼ cup sherry
3 tablespoons butter or margarine

1. Heat oven to 400°F.
2. Scrub yams. Cook according to directions in basic recipe.
3. When cool, peel and place in a single layer in a shallow baking dish.
4. Combine remaining ingredients in a small saucepan and bring just to a boil.
5. Pour sauce over yams.
6. Bake 20 to 25 minutes, basting and turning yams occasionally.
7. Makes 6 to 8 servings.

TOMATOES

Buy large or small red and yellow tomatoes. Look for firm, plump, smooth tomatoes with good color and no blemishes.

Tomatoes are usually served raw or in salads. They also make excellent combinations with a myriad of other dishes.

BROILED TOMATOES PROVENCAL

    3 large tomatoes
1½ tablespoons bottled herb-garlic salad
    dressing
1⅓ cups soft bread crumbs
    ⅓ cup butter or margarine, melted
    1 tablespoon finely chopped parsley
    1 small clove garlic, crushed
    ½ teaspoon salt
    Dash of pepper

1. Cut out stem ends from tomatoes. Cut tomatoes in half crosswise. Brush salad dressing over cut sides of tomatoes.
2. In a small bowl combine remaining ingredients and mix lightly. Spoon evenly over tomato halves.
3. Place on broiler pan. Broil, 5 inches from source of heat, 3 to 4 minutes or until topping is lightly browned.
4. Makes 6 servings.

FRIED TOMATOES

    4 firm ripe or green tomatoes
    Flour
    Salt and pepper
    ¼ cup butter or margarine
    1 tablespoon flour
    ¾ cup milk

1. Wash tomatoes. Remove stem ends. Cut each tomato in 3 or 4 thick slices, crosswise.
2. Mix together 2 tablespoons flour with a little salt and pepper. Dip tomato slices in flour mixture.
3. Heat butter in large skillet. Add tomato slices and cook about 3 minutes, turning to brown both sides. Remove tomato slices to a heated serving platter.
4. Stir flour into fat left in pan and stir until smooth. Stir in milk. Cook over low heat, stirring constantly, until smooth and thickened. Season to taste with salt and pepper. Serve with tomato slices.
5. Makes 4 servings.

TURNIPS AND RUTABAGAS

In the summer turnips are sold in bunches with tops attached; tops should be young, fresh and green. At other times of the year turnips are sold in bags. Turnips should be firm and heavy for their size. Avoid those that are light weight for their size; they may be woody, pithy and strong in flavor. Rutabagas are available during fall, winter and early spring. Buy heavy, firm, and smooth rutabagas with few roots at the ends. Avoid lightweight ones; they may be woody, pithy and strong in flavor.

Scrub vegetables. Pare thinly and cut into small cubes, strips or very thin slices.

1. Place turnips or rutabaga pieces in a pan that they most nearly fill.
2. Add 3 ounces water.
3. Put cover on pan with vac-control valve open.
4. Place over medium-high heat.
5. Allow vapor to escape through vac-control valve 3 to 5 minutes.
6. Close vac-control valve and turn off heat. Do not remove cover.
7. Let stand 20 minutes.
8. Season to taste. Rutabagas are very good mashed and seasoned to taste.
9. 1½ pounds makes 4 servings.

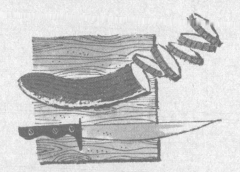

GLAZED TURNIPS

    6 medium turnips
    2 tablespoons butter
    ¼ cup honey
    ¼ cup water
    ¼ teaspoon nutmeg
    ¼ teaspoon salt

1. Peel and dice turnips.
2. Cook according to directions in basic recipe, cutting steaming time by 5 minutes.
3. Heat oven to 350°F.
4. Place drained turnips in a buttered baking dish.
5. Combine butter, honey, water, nutmeg and salt in a small saucepan. Heat until butter melts.
6. Pour combined ingredients over turnips. Bake about 1 hour or until turnips are lightly browned and glazed.
7. Makes about 4 servings.

Sauerbraten

Meats

Most cooks plan their dinners around the main course: meat. It represents a large portion of everyone's food budget, so it is wise to know the best ways to purchase it as well as to cook it in order to receive the most from your meat expenditures. Because you are cooking with utensils which provide a different concept in meat preparation, be sure to read the instructions carefully and follow the step-by-step directions for roasting and for broiling on top of the range. Since no one's budget provides for steaks or roasts daily, many delicious ways to cook less expensive cuts are included.

MEAT KNOW-HOW

All meat processed in plants which sell their products across state lines must, under Federal law, be inspected for wholesomeness. Meat which passes this inspection is stamped with a round mark which bears the legend "U. S. INSP'D & P'S'D." This mark tells you that the meat is clean and wholesome.

In addition, meat is often graded for quality. When the carcass is graded, a purple shield-shaped grade mark containing the letters USDA and the grade name—such as Prime, Choice or Good—is applied with a roller stamp. The grade shield is rolled on in a long ribbon-like imprint along the length of the carcass. When the carcass is divided, one or more of the grade marks will appear on most of these meat cuts.

Because beef can vary so much in quality, it takes eight grades to span the range. However, usually only the first 3 grades are offered to the consumer in the market.

Prime beef is the ultimate in tenderness, juiciness and flavor. It has abundant marbling, flakes of fat within the lean, which enhances both the flavor and juiciness. Prime meat is considered by many as the finest in eating, however, the quantity produced is limited and a comparatively small amount finds its way to the consumer markets.

Choice beef has slightly less marbling than prime, but still is of very high quality. Choice cuts of rib, rump, round and sirloin tip can be roasted. Choice grade is produced in the greatest volume and retailers have found that this level of quality pleases most of their customers.

Good grade beef often pleases thrifty shoppers because it is somewhat more lean than the higher grades. It is relatively tender, but because it has less marbling it lacks some of the juiciness and flavor of the higher grades. Rib, rib eye, rump and sirloin cuts roast nicely; however, other cuts usually do better with moist heat.

TOP STOVE ROASTING

Select chunky, quality cuts of beef, veal, pork or lamb, weighing at least 3 pounds. Use either the 4-quart saucepan, the skillet or the Dutch oven, depending on the size and shape of the roast.

1. Preheat utensil on medium-high heat. Place a small square of butcher's paper or white paper in bottom of pan. When the paper starts to turn brown the utensil is hot. Remove paper.
2. Put the meat in the pan and brown evenly on all sides. When the cold meat hits the hot pan it will stick, but as the meat browns and fat is released from the meat, it will loosen.
3. When roast is browned, cover and reduce heat to medium.
4. When cover is hot to the touch, approximately 3 to 5 minutes, reduce heat to low. Cook to desired degree of doneness, turning once when half done.
5. Refer to the following chart for approximate cooking times for top stove roasting.

Approximate Time Chart for Top Stove Roasting of Meats

Beef	
Rare	15 to 18 minutes per pound
Medium	18 to 20 minutes per pound
Well done	20 to 27 minutes per pound
Ham	30 to 35 minutes per pound
Lamb	
Leg	25 to 30 minutes per pound
Shoulder	40 to 45 minutes per pound
Pork	30 to 35 minutes per pound
Veal	25 to 30 minutes per pound

Note: When roast is turned in middle of roasting period, a meat thermometer may be inserted into the center to judge more accurately the desired degree of doneness.

Pan-Broiled Steak

Place Dutch oven over medium-high heat.
Place a piece of paper in pan. When paper starts to brown, pan is ready.

Remove paper. Place meat in pan. Brown meat well on all sides. Meat will stick to hot pan but will loosen as it cooks.

Cover and reduce heat to medium. When cover is hot to the touch, reduce heat to low. Turn once during cooking time.

Some Meat Cuts Suitable For Top Stove Roasting

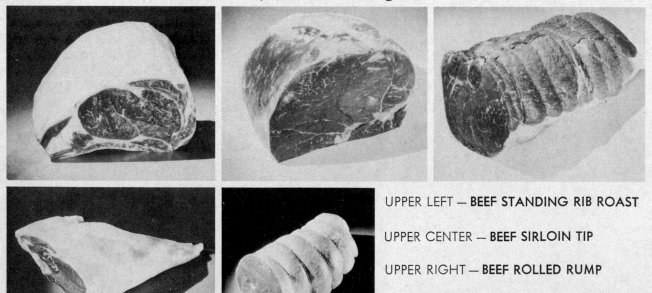

UPPER LEFT — **BEEF STANDING RIB ROAST**

UPPER CENTER — **BEEF SIRLOIN TIP**

UPPER RIGHT — **BEEF ROLLED RUMP**

LOWER LEFT — **LAMB LEG,** SIRLOIN OFF

LOWER RIGHT — **ROLLED BONELESS VEAL**

Veal Scallops with Lemon

Stuffed Pork Chops

PAN-BROILING

The same tender cuts of meat suitable for range broiling, when cut 1-inch thick or less, are excellent pan-broiled.

1. Place skillet over medium-high heat. Place a small square of butcher's paper or white paper in bottom of pan. When paper turns brown the skillet is hot. Remove paper.
2. If meat has fat on edges, slash at 1-inch intervals to prevent curling during cooking.
3. Place meat in skillet and brown well on both sides. When cold meat hits the hot pan it will stick, but as the meat browns and fat is released from the meat, it will loosen.
4. Reduce heat to low. Do not cover.
5. Pour off fat as it accumulates in bottom of pan.
6. Continue cooking to desired degree of doneness. Count on roughly half the time for pan-broiling as is required for broiling in the oven. To test for doneness, cut a small gash close to bone near the end of the cooking time and note the color of the meat.
7. Season to taste and serve immediately.

Some Meat Cuts Suitable For Panbroiling and Panfrying

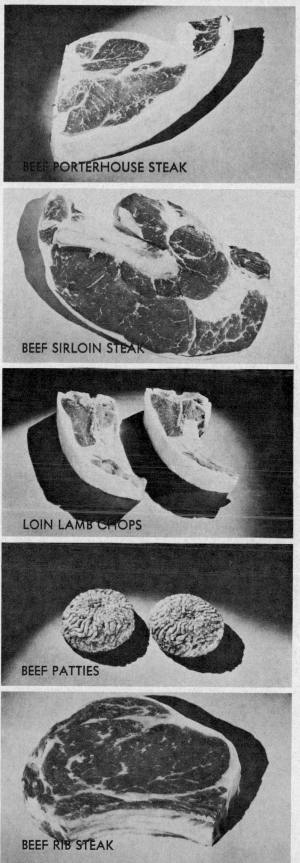

BEEF PORTERHOUSE STEAK

BEEF SIRLOIN STEAK

LOIN LAMB CHOPS

BEEF PATTIES

BEEF RIB STEAK

Place skillet over medium-high heat. Place a piece of paper in skillet. When paper starts to brown, pan is ready.

Remove paper. Place meat in pan. Meat will stick to hot pan but will loosen as it cooks. Cook to desired degree of taste.

PAN-FRYING

When a small amount of fat is added before, or allowed to accumulate during cooking, the method is called pan-frying. Comparatively thin pieces of tender meat, or those made tender by pounding, scoring, cubing or grinding may be pan-fried.

1. Heat skillet over medium-high heat. If there is fat on meat, do not add fat. Other meats low in fat, such as cubed steaks and cuts which are floured or breaded, require additional fat to cover the surface of the frying pan and prevent sticking.
2. Place meat in hot skillet and brown one side. Turn and brown other side.
3. Do not cover. Do not add water.
4. Season to taste and serve immediately.

Approximate Time Chart for Pan-Frying

Meat	Thickness	Weight	Time in minutes
Frozen sandwich-type steaks		3 to 8 ounces	3
Liver	¼-inch		10 to 12
Club, rib or tenderloin steak	½- to ¾-inch		10 to 20 (rare to medium)
Hamburgers	¾-inch	4 ounces	12 to 20 (rare to medium)
Cube steaks	¼-inch	4 ounces	4 to 8

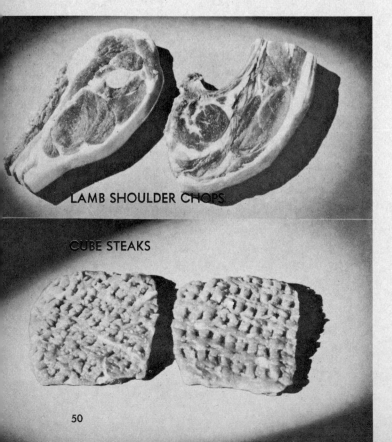

LAMB SHOULDER CHOPS

CUBE STEAKS

BRAISING

This method of cooking is suitable for less tender cuts of meat. Some tender cuts also can be braised, such as pork steaks and cutlets, veal chops, steaks and cutlets, and pork liver.

1. Place skillet or Dutch oven over medium-high heat. Place a small square of butcher's paper or white paper in bottom of pan. When paper turns brown the utensil is hot. Remove paper.
2. Reduce heat to medium and brown meat well on all sides. Pour off drippings as meat browns.
3. Season with salt, pepper, herbs and spices, if desired.
4. Add a small amount of liquid, if necessary. Liquid is usually added to less tender cuts but may be omitted when cooking tender cuts such as pork chops and pork tenderloin.
5. Cover, with vac-control valve open, allow vapor to escape in a steady stream through vac-control valve.
6. Close vac-control valve and reduce heat to low. Simmer until tender.
7. Use liquid left in pan for pan gravy.

COOKING IN LIQUID

Large, less tender cuts of meat and stews are prepared by cooking in liquid.

LARGE CUTS

1. Heat Dutch oven over medium-high heat. Place a small amount of fat in Dutch oven. Brown meat well on all sides.
2. Cover the meat with water, stock or other liquid. By covering the meat with liquid, uniform cooking is assured.
3. Season with salt, pepper, herbs, spices and vegetables as desired.
4. Cover Dutch oven with vac-control valve closed. Simmer, do not boil, over low heat until meat is tender.
5. When vegetables are to be cooked with the meat, as in a boiled dinner, add them whole or in pieces, just long enough before the meat is tender, to cook them.

Note: When preparing Corned Beef or a Boiled Dinner, do not brown first. Start with step No. 2.

STEWS

1. Cut meat in uniform pieces, usually 1- to 2-inch cubes.
2. Heat Dutch oven over medium-high heat. Add a small amount of fat to Dutch oven. Add meat cubes and brown well on all sides.
3. Add just enough liquid to cover meat.
4. Season to taste.
5. Cover Dutch oven with vac-control valve closed. Simmer, do not boil, over low heat until meat is tender.
6. Add vegetables to the meat just long enough before serving to be cooked.

BEEF BLADE POT ROAST

STEW MEAT

BEEF HEEL OF ROUND

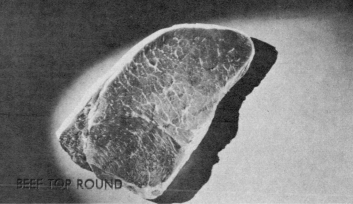

BEEF TOP ROUND

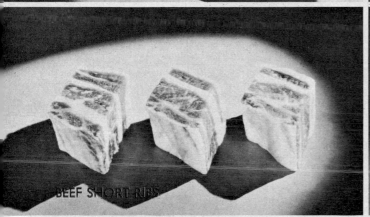

BEEF SHORT RIBS

LAMB SHANK

Some Meat Cuts Suitable For Braising and Cooking In Liquid

BEEF FLANK STEAK

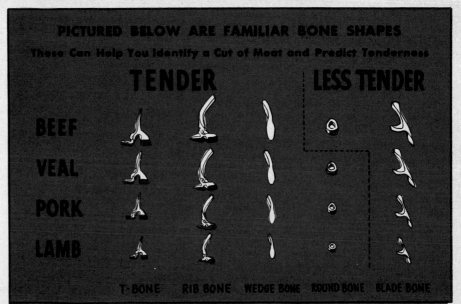

PICTURED BELOW ARE FAMILIAR BONE SHAPES
These Can Help You Identify a Cut of Meat and Predict Tenderness

	TENDER			LESS TENDER	
BEEF					
VEAL					
PORK					
LAMB					
	T-BONE	RIB BONE	WEDGE BONE	ROUND BONE	BLADE BONE

BEEF

RIBS OF BEEF

1. Select a rib of beef with at least 2 ribs. Have butcher remove short ribs. Remove as much fat as possible.
2. Place Dutch oven or skillet over medium-high heat. Place a piece of butcher's paper or white paper in pan. When paper starts to turn brown the utensil is hot. Remove paper.
3. Put ribs of beef in the pan and brown evenly on all sides. When the cold meat hits the hot pan it will stick, but as the meat browns and fat is released from the meat, it will loosen.
4. When the meat is browned (this will take 20 to 30 minutes), cover and reduce heat to medium.
5. When cover is hot to the touch (after approximately 3 to 5 minutes), reduce heat to low. Cook to desired degree of doneness, turning once when half done.
6. Ribs of beef take a shorter cooking time than chunky cuts of beef. After browning, roast 10 to 12 minutes per pound for rare beef, 13 to 15 minutes per pound for medium beef, 15 to 20 minutes per pound for well-done beef.

ROAST BEEF

1. Select a chunky piece of meat such as rolled ribs, sirloin roast or eye round. The roast should weigh at least 3 pounds.
2. Depending on size of meat, preheat either the Dutch oven, skillet or 4-quart saucepan over medium-high heat until a square of butcher's paper or white paper, placed in the bottom of the pan, starts to turn brown.
3. Place meat in pan and brown well on all sides. When the cold meat hits the hot pan it will stick, but as the meat browns and fat is released from the meat, it will loosen.
4. When meat is browned, cover and reduce heat to medium.
5. When cover is hot to the touch, after approximately 3 to 5 minutes, reduce heat to low. As the meat roasts, it should crackle and spit in the pan. If there is no sound, raise heat slightly.
6. Turn meat once when half-cooked and season with salt and pepper.
7. Roast 15 to 18 minutes per pound for rare beef, 18 to 20 minutes per pound for medium beef, 20 to 27 minutes per pound for well-done beef.

POT ROAST

3 to 4 pounds beef pot roast
2 teaspoons salt
¼ teaspoon pepper
1 medium onion, sliced
½ cup water
6 carrots, scraped and cut in chunks
6 medium potatoes, peeled and cut in chunks
6 small onions, peeled

1. Pre-heat Dutch oven over medium-high heat according to directions for top stove roasting. Brown pot roast well on all sides.
2. Sprinkle with salt and pepper. Add onion and water. Cover with vac-control valve closed. Reduce heat and simmer 2½ to 3 hours, or until meat is very tender when pierced with a fork. Turn pot roast once during cooking time.
3. About 45 minutes before pot roast is cooked add carrots, potatoes and onions.
4. Remove pot roast to a hot serving platter. Cut in slices and serve with strained juices from the Dutch oven.
5. Makes 4 to 6 servings.

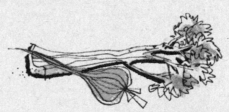

GEOFF'S POT ROAST

3 pound pot roast, cross rib or chuck
1 large onion, chopped
½ green pepper, chopped
1 cup catsup
1 teaspoon salt
¼ teaspoon pepper
1 teaspoon Worcestershire sauce
½ teaspoon prepared mustard

1. Preheat Dutch oven over medium-high heat until a square of paper in the bottom turns brown. Remove paper.
2. Brown beef in hot Dutch oven until well browned on all sides.
3. Add onion and green pepper and cook about 3 minutes.
4. Add remaining ingredients.
5. Cover with vac-control valve closed. Reduce heat to low.
6. Cook over low heat about 3 hours or until meat is tender, turning meat occasionally. If mixture gets too thick during cooking, add a small amount of water.
7. Makes 6 to 8 servings.

SAUERBRATEN

1½ cups vinegar
1½ cups water
2 bay leaves
12 whole cloves
¼ teaspoon pepper
¼ teaspoon mace
1½ teaspoon salt
1 tablespoon sugar
2 large onions, sliced
¼ cup salad oil
3 to 4 pound heel of round beef
½ cup flour, divided
3 tablespoons shortening
½ cup gingersnap crumbs

1. Combine vinegar, water, bay leaves, cloves, pepper, mace, salt, sugar and onions in a large saucepan. Bring to a boil. Cool and stir in salad oil.
2. Place meat in a deep bowl. Pour vinegar mixture over meat. Place in refrigerator. Let stand 2 to 4 days, turning meat once a day so it will marinate evenly.
3. Remove meat from marinade and pat dry with paper towels. Cover surface of meat with ¼ cup flour.
4. Heat shortening in Dutch oven over medium-high heat. Add beef and brown well on all sides.
5. Strain marinade. Add 1 cup strained marinade to beef.
6. Cover with vac-control valve closed and simmer over low heat 3 to 4 hours or until meat is fork tender. Turn meat occasionally.
7. Remove meat to a hot serving platter. Add enough strained marinade to Dutch oven to make 2 cups liquid. Combine remaining flour with ¼ cup cold marinade and stir until smooth. Stir into liquid in pan. Bring to a boil, stirring constantly, and cook until smooth and thickened. Stir in gingersnap crumbs and heat thoroughly. Season to taste.
8. Slice beef and serve with gravy.
9. Makes 6 to 8 servings.

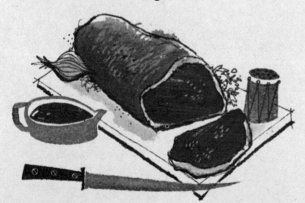

STEAK DIANE

4 sirloin strip steaks, cut ½ inch thick
Salt
Freshly ground black pepper
1 teaspoon dry mustard
¼ cup butter or margarine
3 tablespoons lemon juice
2 teaspoons snipped chives
1 teaspoon Worcestershire sauce

1. With a meat mallet or the bottom of a heavy saucepan, pound steaks to ⅓-inch thickness. Sprinkle one side of steak with salt, pepper and ⅛ teaspoon of the dry mustard. Pound mixture into meat. Repeat on other side of meat.
2. Melt butter in skillet over medum-high heat.
3. When butter is very hot add steaks and cook 2 minutes on each side. Remove steaks to a hot serving platter.
4. To drippings in skillet add lemon juice, chives, Worcestershire sauce and remaining mustard. Bring to boil. Pour over meat.
5. Makes 4 servings.

Note: For a very special party touch, Steak Diane may be prepared at the dinner table in a chafing dish or electric skillet.

SWISS STEAK

2 pounds round steak, cut 1 inch thick
⅓ cup flour
¾ teaspoon salt
¼ teaspoon pepper
3 tablespoons cooking oil
1 can (1 pound 12 ounces) tomatoes
¼ teaspoon sugar
2 tablespoons finely chopped onions

1. Cut steak into 6 or 8 pieces.
2. Combine flour, salt, and pepper. Pound flour mixture into both sides of round steak with a meat hammer, dull side of a knife, or edge of a saucer.
3. Heat oil in skillet over medium-high heat. Brown pieces of meat in hot oil.
4. Add tomatoes, sugar and onion.
5. Cover with vac-control valve closed. Cook over low heat 1 to 1½ hours or until meat is tender.
6. Makes 6 to 8 servings.

ORIENTAL CHUCK STEAK

2 tablespoons fat
3 pound chuck steak, cut 1¼ inches thick
2 medium onions, sliced
    Water
1 can (8 ounces) bamboo shoots, drained; reserve liquid
¼ cup soy sauce
1 tablespoon molasses
1 beef bouillon cube
1 cup diagonally sliced celery
1 jar (2 ounces) sliced pimiento
1 tablespoon cornstarch
2 tablespoons cold water

1. Heat fat in skillet over medium-high heat.
2. Brown chuck steak on both sides in hot fat.
3. Add onions and cook until golden brown.
4. Add water to drained bamboo-shoot liquid to make ¾ cup liquid. Combine liquid with soy sauce, molasses, and bouillon cube. Add to meat.
5. Cover with vac-control valve closed. Cook over low heat about 1 hour, or until meat is nearly tender.
6. Add bamboo shoots, celery and pimiento. Continue cooking until celery is crisply tender, about 25 minutes.
7. Remove meat and vegetables to a hot serving platter.
8. Spoon off as much fat as possible from drippings in skillet. Add water to drippings if necessary to make 1 cup of liquid.
9. Combine cornstarch and water. Stir into liquid in skillet. Cook, stirring constantly, until mixture is smooth and thickened. Serve with meat and vegetables.
10. Makes 6 servings.

STUFFED FLANK STEAK

2 tablespoons butter or margarine
⅓ cup chopped onion
2 hard-cooked eggs, chopped
1 cup dairy sour cream
2 cups packaged herb-flavored stuffing
½ cup hot water
1 egg, beaten
1 flank steak
    Meat tenderizer
2 tablespoons fat

1. Melt butter in skillet over medium heat.
2. Add onions and cook until tender but not browned.
3. Remove skillet from heat and scrape onions into a mixing bowl. Add chopped eggs, ¼ cup of the sour cream, stuffing, water and beaten egg. Mix well.

4. Pound steak with the back of a cleaver or the edge of a saucer on both sides, until it is a thin rectangle. Use tenderizer according to package directions.
5. Spread stuffing mixture over meat. Roll up as for a jelly roll. Tie every 3 to 4 inches with stout cord or secure with skewers.
6. Melt fat in skillet over medium-high heat. Place flank steak in skillet and brown well on all sides.
7. Add ½ cup hot water.
8. Cover with vac-control valve closed. Lower heat and simmer about 1½ hours or until meat is tender.
9. Remove meat to a hot serving platter. Measure drippings in pan and add enough water to make ½ cup liquid. Return to pan. Stir in remaining sour cream and heat but do not boil.
10. Cut flank steak in crosswise slices and serve with hot sauce.
11. Makes 4 servings.

ROUND STEAK BIRDS

2 pounds round steak, cut ½-inch thick
2 tablespoons flour
1 teaspoon salt
8 carrot strips
8 celery strips
4 dill pickles, cut in half lengthwise
3 tablespoons fat
1 cup beef bouillon
¼ teaspoon pepper
¼ teaspoon onion salt

1. Cut round steak in 8 pieces, about 3 by 4 inches. Pound flour into meat with edge of heavy saucer or back of heavy knife. Sprinkle salt on meat. Lay one strip each of carrot, celery and pickle on each piece of meat. Fold meat over and fasten with a toothpick.
2. Brown meat in hot fat in skillet over medium high heat.
3. Add remaining ingredients.
4. Cover with vac-control valve closed and simmer over low heat about 1¼ hours or until meat is tender.
5. Makes 6 to 8 servings.

MOUNT VERNON SHORT RIBS

¼ cup flour
1 teaspoon salt
¼ teaspoon pepper
4 pounds beef short ribs, cut into 3-inch pieces
2 tablespoons butter or margarine
2 medium onions, chopped
¼ cup molasses
¼ cup catsup
3 tablespoons vinegar
1 can (12 ounces) beer or ale
½ teaspoon Tabasco
6 carrots, scrubbed or peeled and cut in thirds

1. Combine flour, salt and pepper. Place in a paper bag. Add short ribs and shake until ribs are coated with flour mixture.
2. Place butter in Dutch oven and heat over medium-high heat.
3. Add ribs and brown well on all sides.
4. Remove ribs. Add onion and cook until tender but not browned.
5. Add molasses, catsup, vinegar, beer and Tabasco. Mix well. Return short ribs to Dutch oven.
6. Cover with vac-control valve closed. Cook over low heat 1½ to 2 hours, or until ribs are almost tender.
7. Add carrots and cook 15 to 20 minutes longer or until carrots are tender.
8. Makes 5 to 6 servings.

CHINESE PEPPER STEAK

1 pound round steak
¼ cup salad oil
1 clove garlic
½ cup coarsely chopped onion
2 cups bite-size pieces green pepper
1 teaspoon salt
¼ teaspoon pepper
¼ teaspoon ginger
1 tablespoon cornstarch
1 cup stock or bouillon
1 tablespoon soy sauce
Hot cooked rice

1. Cut steak diagonally across the grain into thin slices, then cut into strips about 2 inches long.
2. Heat salad oil in skillet over medium heat. Place garlic clove and meat in oil and cook over medium heat, turning as needed, until browned. Remove garlic and discard.
3. Add onion, green pepper, salt, pepper and ginger. Cook over medium heat, stirring constantly, until just tender.
4. Combine cornstarch with stock and soy sauce. Stir into mixture in skillet. Bring to a boil and cook, stirring constantly, until mixture becomes thick and clear.
5. Serve immediately over hot cooked rice.
6. Makes about 4 servings.

ROUND STEAK STROGANOFF

1½ pound round steak
   Meat tenderizer
¼ cup butter or margarine
2 tablespoons flour
1 cup beef bouillon
½ cup dry red wine
1 tablespoon instant minced onion
1 can (4 ounces) sliced mushrooms
   Salt and pepper
½ cup dairy sour cream
   Hot buttered noodles or rice

1. Cut steak across the grain into thin strips ½ inch x 2 inches. Sprinkle with meat tenderizer according to package directions. Let stand.
2. Melt 2 tablespoons butter in a skillet over medium-high heat. Add steak and brown gently. Remove meat from skillet.
3. Melt remaining butter in skillet. Stir in flour to make a smooth paste. Stir in bouillon, red wine, and onions. Drain mushrooms and add mushroom liquid. Cook over medium heat, stirring constantly, until smooth and thickened. Season to taste with salt and pepper.
4. Return meat to sauce. Add mushrooms.
5. Cover, with vac-control valve closed. Lower heat and simmer gently about 30 minutes, or until meat is tender.
6. Stir in sour cream and heat but do not boil.
7. Serve with hot noodles or rice.
8. Makes about 4 servings.

BAVARIAN STEW

2 pounds beef chuck or stew meat
3 tablespoons butter or margarine
2 medium onions, sliced
3 cups hot water
1 bay leaf
3 teaspoons salt
¼ teaspoon black pepper
1½ teaspoons caraway seed
¼ cup vinegar
1 medium-sized head red cabbage
½ cup gingersnap crumbs

1. Cut beef into 1½- to 2-inch cubes.
2. Melt butter in Dutch oven over medium-high heat. Brown beef cubes in hot butter on all sides. Add onions and brown for 3 minutes. Add water, bay leaf, salt, pepper and caraway seed.
3. Cover tightly with vac-control valve closed. Reduce heat to low. Simmer about 1½ hours or until meat is almost tender.
4. Cut cabbage in wedges. Place cabbage on top of stew meat. Cover tightly and simmer 25 to 30 minutes or until cabbage is tender.
5. Meanwhile, soak gingersnap crumbs in ¼ cup of warm water.
6. Remove cabbage and meat from Dutch oven and place on a deep serving plate.
7. Add gingersnap crumbs to gravy in pan and cook, stirring constantly, until gravy is smooth and thickened.
8. Pour gravy over meat and serve with boiled buttered noodles.
9. Makes 6 servings.

HUNGARIAN GOULASH

1 tablespoon flour
1 teaspoon Ac'cent
1½ pounds boneless beef chuck, cut in 1-inch cubes
3 tablespoons butter or margarine
2 cups thinly sliced onions
2 teaspoons salt
4 teaspoons paprika
2½ cups water
Hot buttered noodles

1. Combine flour and Ac'cent. Toss pieces of meat in flour mixture to coat all sides.
2. Melt butter in a skillet over medium-high heat. Add beef and brown thoroughly on all sides. Add onions, salt, paprika and water.
3. Cover with vac-control valve closed. Lower heat and simmer about 2 hours or until fork tender.
4. Serve over hot buttered noodles.
5. Makes 6 servings.

OLD FASHIONED BEEF STEW

1 teaspoon salt, divided
2 teaspoons Ac'cent
⅛ teaspoon pepper
¼ cup flour
2 pounds boneless stewing beef, cut into 1½-inch cubes
¼ cup butter or margarine
3 cups water
2 celery stalks with leaves, finely cut
1 bay leaf
12 small white onions, peeled
6 medium carrots, scraped and halved
3 medium potatoes, thinly peeled and halved

1. Blend together ½ teaspoon salt, Ac'cent, pepper and flour. Toss pieces of meat in flour mixture. Reserve left-over flour.
2. Melt butter in a Dutch oven over medium-high heat. Add beef and brown thoroughly on all sides. Add water, ½ teaspoon salt, finely cut celery and bay leaf.
3. Cover tightly, with vac-control valve closed. Lower heat and simmer about 2 hours or until meat is almost tender.
4. Add onions, carrots, and potatoes. Cover and simmer until vegetables are tender.
5. Measure reserved flour. If necessary, add enough additional flour to make 2 tablespoons. Combine with 3 tablespoons water and stir to a smooth paste. Gradually add to stew and cook, stirring constantly, until gravy is smooth and thickened.
6. Makes 6 servings.

SOUR CREAM SAUCE BURGERS

1 pound ground beef
1 teaspoon salt
¼ teaspoon pepper
2 tablespoons butter
½ cup sliced green onions
1 cup sliced fresh mushrooms
1 cup dairy sour cream
1 tablespoon chopped parsley

1. Toss together with a fork the beef, salt, and pepper. Shape into 4 thick patties.
2. Melt butter in a saucepan. Add onions and mushrooms and cook until onions are limp but not browned. Reduce heat to very low. Add sour cream and parsley. Salt to taste. Keep warm but do not boil.
3. Heat skillet over medium-high heat. Place patties in hot skillet and fry on both sides to the desired degree of doneness.
4. Serve with hot sour cream sauce.
5. Makes 4 servings.

SWISS BEEF STEW

2 tablespoons salad oil
2 pounds boneless beef chuck, cut into 1-inch cubes
1 tablespoon paprika
6 tablespoons water
1 envelope (1⅝ ounces) Swiss style golden onion soup mix
2 cups water
1 can (10½ ounces) tomato puree
4 medium potatoes, thinly peeled and cubed

1. Heat salad oil in a Dutch oven over medium-high heat. Add beef and brown thoroughly on all sides, turning occasionally.
2. Sprinkle with paprika. Add 6 tablespoons water.
3. Cover tightly with vac-control valve closed. Lower heat and simmer 45 minutes.
4. Stir in onion soup mix, 2 cups of water and tomato puree. Cover tightly and simmer 15 minutes.
5. Add potatoes. Cover tightly and simmer 15 minutes or until potatoes are tender.
6. Makes 4 to 6 servings.

WINE-MUSHROOM HAMBURGERS

1 pound ground beef
¼ cup cream
¼ cup milk
1 tablespoon minced onion
1 teaspoon salt
¼ teaspoon pepper
2 tablespoons butter or margarine
2 tablespoons flour
½ cup beef bouillon
½ cup dry red wine
1 teaspoon Worcestershire sauce
2 tablespoons chopped parsley
1 can (4 ounces) sliced mushrooms
3 or 4 slices toast

1. Combine beef, cream, milk, onion, salt, and pepper. Toss lightly with a fork until blended. Shape into 3 or 4 thick patties.
2. Melt butter in skillet over medium-high heat. Add patties and brown well on both sides. Remove patties and keep warm.
3. Add flour to drippings in pan and stir to blend well. Add bouillon and wine. Cook, stirring constantly, until mixture boils and becomes thick. Add Worcestershire sauce, parsley, and mushrooms with liquid. Taste; add salt and pepper if needed.
4. Return patties to sauce. Simmer over low heat until meat is cooked to desired degree of doneness.
5. Place meat patties on toast slices and pour sauce over the top.
6. Makes 3 or 4 servings.

MEAT LOAF

1 can (8 ounces) tomato sauce
¼ cup brown sugar
¼ cup vinegar
1 teaspoon prepared mustard
1 egg, beaten
1 medium onion, minced
¼ cup cracker crumbs
2 pounds ground chuck
1½ teaspoons salt
¼ teaspoon pepper

1. In a small bowl combine tomato sauce, brown sugar, vinegar, and mustard. Set aside for later.
2. Beat egg in a large mixing bowl. Add onion, cracker crumbs, ground chuck, salt and pepper. Add ½ cup of the tomato mixture and blend thoroughly.
3. Shape mixture into a loaf.
4. Place meat loaf in skillet. Cover with vac-control valve closed.
5. Place skillet over low heat and bake 1 hour.
6. When meat loaf is done, loosen meat loaf from pan with broad spatula. Lift from pan and place on serving platter.
7. Put remaining tomato sauce in a small saucepan and heat. Serve with meat loaf.
8. Makes 8 servings.

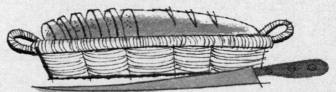

CHILI

2 tablespoons butter or margarine
2 medium onions, chopped
1 clove garlic, minced
1 pound ground chuck
1 teaspoon salt
¼ teaspoon pepper
1 tablespoon chili powder
1 can (1 pound 14 ounces) tomatoes
1 can (1 pound) red kidney beans

1. Melt butter in Dutch oven over medium-high heat. Add onions and garlic and cook, stirring occasionally, until lightly browned.
2. Remove onions and set aside. Add chuck and cook, stirring, until well browned.
3. Add salt, pepper and chili powder. Return onions and garlic to pan. Add tomatoes.
4. Cover with vac-control valve closed. Lower heat and simmer about 30 minutes.
5. Add beans. Cover and simmer about 15 minutes.
6. Makes 4 servings.

BURGUNDY BEEF BALLS

2 tablespoons instant minced onion
¾ cup milk
2 eggs
2 teaspoons salt
¼ teaspoon pepper
1 teaspoon mustard
  Dash of nutmeg
  Dash of allspice
2 cups soft bread crumbs
2 pounds lean ground beef
3 tablespoons shortening
3 tablespoons flour
1 can (10½ ounces) condensed consomme
¾ cup red dinner wine
½ cup dairy sour cream

1. Combine instant minced onion and milk and let stand while preparing remaining ingredients.
2. Beat eggs lightly; add seasonings, crumbs, milk, and onion. Add beef and mix lightly but thoroughly.
3. Shape meat into small balls.
4. Heat shortening in skillet over medium heat.
5. Brown meat balls lightly on all sides. Remove meat balls.
6. Stir flour into drippings. Stir in consomme and wine and cook, stirring constantly, until mixture comes to a boil and is slightly thickened.
7. Return meat balls to skillet.
8. Cover with vac-control valve closed. Cook over low heat 15 minutes.
9. Just before serving add sour cream and mix gently. Heat thoroughly but do not boil.
10. Makes 8 to 10 servings.

MEAT BALL STEW

1 pound small white onions
6 small carrots
1½ pounds ground beef
1 egg, beaten
⅓ cup uncooked rice
½ teaspoon dried thyme
2 teaspoons salt
2 teaspoons Worcestershire sauce
3 cans (8 ounces each) tomato sauce with mushrooms
1 teaspoon curry powder
¾ cup water

1. Remove ends and skins from onions.
2. Cook onions according to directions in vegetable chapter until almost tender. Drain.
3. Scrub carrots and scrape or peel if necessary. Cut in half and cook according to directions in vegetable chapter, until almost tender. Drain.

4. Combine beef, egg, rice, thyme, salt, Worcestershire sauce and ½ can of tomato sauce. Blend lightly but thoroughly. Shape mixture into small balls.
5. Preheat Dutch oven over medium-high heat until a square of butcher's or white paper in the bottom turns brown. Remove paper.
6. Place meat balls in Dutch oven and brown on all sides.
7. Add partially cooked vegetables to Dutch oven.
8. Cover, with vac-control valve closed. Cook over low heat 25 to 30 minutes, or until vegetables are tender and meat balls cooked.
10. Makes 4 to 6 servings.

MEAT BALLS DEL VINO

2 slices day-old bread
2 tablespoons water
1½ pounds ground beef
2 eggs, beaten
1½ tablespoons grated onion
1½ teaspoons salt
¼ teaspoon pepper
3 tablespoons fat
¼ cup butter or margarine
¼ cup flour
2 tablespoons prepared mustard
2 cups beef bouillon
¼ cup dry red table wine

1. Cut bread in tiny cubes. Moisten with water.
2. Combine beef, eggs, onion, salt and pepper. Add soaked bread and blend mixture lightly but thoroughly.
3. Form mixture into 48 small meat balls.
4. Melt fat in skillet over medium heat.
5. Brown meat balls on all sides in hot fat.
6. Remove meat balls from skillet and pour off excess drippings.
7. Melt butter in skillet. Blend in flour and mustard.
8. Remove skillet from heat and stir in bouillon. Cook over medium heat, stirring constantly, until mixture comes to a boil and is thickened.
9. Return meat balls to sauce.
10. Cover with vac-control valve closed. Cook over low heat 15 minutes.
11. Just before serving, stir in wine.
12. Makes 6 to 8 servings.

SWEDISH MEAT BALLS

2 cups fresh bread cubes
½ cup milk
1 onion, finely chopped
¼ cup butter
3 eggs, beaten
1 teaspoon salt
¼ teaspoon pepper
2 teaspoons paprika
2 teaspoons ground nutmeg
1 teaspoon dry mustard
1½ pounds ground chuck
1 teaspoon mixed herbs
1 clove garlic, minced
1 teaspoon meat concentrate
2 teaspoons tomato paste
¼ cup flour
2 cups beef bouillon
2 cups dairy sour cream

1. Combine bread cubes and milk and let stand.
2. Cook onion in 1 tablespoon of the butter over medium heat until tender, but not browned.
3. Squeeze as much milk out of the bread as possible and place bread in a mixing bowl. Add the cooked onion, eggs, salt, pepper, paprika, nutmeg and mustard. Blend thoroughly. Add chuck and mixed herbs and blend thoroughly with the hands until well mixed.
4. Shape meat mixture into 1-inch balls.
5. Heat remaining 3 tablespoons butter in a skillet over medium high heat. Brown meat balls, a few at a time, on all sides. As meat balls are cooked, remove from skillet.
6. Cook garlic in meat drippings for 1 minute. Add meat concentrate, tomato paste and flour and stir well.
7. Stir in beef bouillon. Cook over medium heat, stirring constantly, until mixture comes to a boil and thickens.
8. Lower heat and stir in sour cream. Heat but do not boil.
9. Return meat balls to pan and simmer over low heat until meat balls are well heated.
10. Serve with hot buttered noodles, if desired.
11. Makes 6 to 8 servings.

BEEF BALL CASSEROLE

1 package (8 ounces) elbow macaroni
1 pound ground beef
¾ teaspoon salt
⅛ teaspoon pepper
1 can (6 ounces) sliced, broiled-in-butter mushrooms
2 tablespoons butter or margarine
½ cup chopped celery
½ cup chopped onions
1 can (1 pound) whole baby carrots
Milk
1 can (10½ ounces) condensed mushroom soup
Seasoned bread crumbs
Butter

1. Heat oven to 375°F.
2. Cook macaroni according to package directions. Drain in colander. Set aside.
3. Combine beef, salt and pepper. Shape mixture into 1-inch balls.
4. Drain mushrooms and reserve liquid.
5. Melt butter in a skillet over medium heat. Add mushrooms, celery and onion. Cook about 3 minutes and remove from skillet.
6. Brown meat balls on all sides in skillet.
7. Drain carrots and reserve liquid. Combine reserved liquids with enough milk to measure 1¼ cups liquid. Stir reserved liquids and milk into mushroom soup. Combine with mushrooms, celery and onions. Blend lightly. Add meat balls and carrots.
8. Turn mixture into a 2½-quart casserole. Sprinkle top with bread crumbs and dot with butter.
9. Bake 20 to 25 minutes or until hot and bubbly.
10. Makes 6 servings.

SWEET-AND-SOUR POT ROAST

1 tablespoon shortening
3 pound round-bone pot roast
¼ cup sliced onions
½ cup vinegar
⅓ cup brown sugar
⅛ teaspoon nutmeg
¼ teaspoon salt

1. Melt shortening in Dutch oven over medium-high heat. Add pot roast and brown well on on all sides.
2. Remove meat and cook onions until limp and transparent.
3. Return meat to Dutch oven. Add remaining ingredients.
4. Cover with vac-control valve closed. Simmer over low heat about 2½ to 3 hours or until meat is tender.
5. Makes 4 to 5 servings.

BARBECUED POT ROAST

3 to 4 pound beef pot roast
3 tablespoons fat
1 teaspoon salt
⅛ teaspoon pepper
½ cup catsup
½ cup water
1 tablespoon vinegar
1 tablespoon brown sugar
2 tablespoons lemon juice
1 tablespoon Worcestershire sauce
1 medium onion, sliced

1. Preheat Dutch oven over medium-high heat until a square of butcher's paper or white paper in the bottom turns brown. Remove paper.
2. Brown beef in hot fat until well browned on on all sides.
3. Pour off drippings.
4. Combine remaining ingredients. Pour over meat.
5. Cover with vac-control valve closed. Reduce heat to low.
6. Cook over low heat 3 to 3½ hours or until meat is tender.
7. Makes 6 to 8 servings.

BEEF GOULASH

¼ cup salad oil
3 pounds boneless beef chuck, cut into 1½-inch cubes
4 medium onions, finely chopped
1½ cups water
¼ cup tomato paste
¼ cup chopped parsley
2 teaspoons salt
1 teaspoon thyme
¼ teaspoon pepper

1. Heat oil in Dutch oven over medium-high heat. Put half of the beef cubes in Dutch oven and brown well on all sides. Remove from Dutch oven and add remaining beef cubes. Brown well. Remove from Dutch oven.
2. Add onion to drippings in Dutch oven and cook until golden brown. Return browned meat to pan.
3. Stir in water, tomato paste, parsley, salt, thyme and pepper.
4. Cover with vac-control valve closed. Reduce heat to low and cook 1½ to 2 hours, or until beef is tender. Stir occasionally during cooking period.
5. Makes 8 servings.

CREAMY BEEF

1½ pounds lean beef
¼ cup flour
1 teaspoon salt
⅛ teaspoon pepper
2 tablespoons butter or margarine
1 cup sliced onions
1 clove garlic, minced
2 teaspoons Worcestershire sauce
2 tablespoons tomato catsup
1 can (8 ounces) button mushrooms
¾ cup buttermilk

1. Cut beef into strips 2″ long, ¼ to ½ inch thick.
2. Combine flour, salt, and pepper in a paper bag.
3. Add beef strips and shake until beef is coated with flour mixture.
4. Melt butter in a large skillet over medium-high heat.
5. Add beef and brown slowly.
6. When beef is brown on all sides, add onion, garlic, Worcestershire sauce and catsup.
7. Drain liquid from mushrooms and add to meat.
8. Cover, with vac-control valve closed. Reduce heat to low. Cook over low heat about 1 hour, or until meat is tender.
9. Add mushrooms and buttermilk and cook over low heat, stirring, only until mixture is heated through.
10. Serve over hot buttered noodles or rice.
11. Makes 4 to 5 servings.

BARBADOS BEEF STEW

3 pounds beef chuck, cut in 1½-inch cubes
3 tablespoons flour
1 tablespoon fat
1 can (1 pound) tomatoes
2 medium onions, sliced
1 teaspoon salt
1 teaspoon celery salt
¼ teaspoon pepper
⅓ cup cider vinegar
⅓ cup molasses
1 cup water
6 carrots, pared and cut in pieces
½ cup raisins
½ teaspoon ginger

1. Sprinkle beef cubes with flour.
2. Melt fat in Dutch oven over medium-high heat. Add beef cubes and brown well on all sides.

3. Add tomatoes, onions, salt, celery salt, and pepper.
4. Combine vinegar, molasses and water. Add to meat.
5. Cover, with vac-control valve closed. Reduce heat to low.
6. Cook over low heat about 2 hours, stirring occasionally.
7. Add carrots, raisins and ginger.
8. Cook over low heat until carrots are tender.
9. Serve with mashed potatoes or hot cooked rice.
10. Makes 12 servings.

Note: Left-over stew may be packed into freezer containers; be sure to leave 1-inch space on top for expansion. Place in freezer and freeze. To serve, remove from container and place in saucepan. Warm over very low heat, stirring occasionally.

CHINESE BEEF AND VEGETABLES

1 pound round steak
¼ cup salad oil
1 cup green pepper strips
1 cup thinly sliced celery
1 cup sliced fresh mushrooms
½ cup coarsely chopped onion
1 can (1 pound) bean sprouts, drained
1 can (5 ounces) water chestnuts, drained and sliced
1 teaspoon salt
¼ teaspoon ginger
⅛ teaspoon pepper
1½ tablespoons cornstarch
1 cup bouillon
1 tablespoon soy sauce

1. Cut steak diagonally across the grain into very thin slices, then cut into strips 2 inches long.
2. Heat salad oil in skillet over medium-high heat. Add meat and brown well on all sides.
3. Add green peppers, celery, mushrooms, onion, bean sprouts, water chestnuts, salt, ginger, and pepper. Cook, stirring constantly, just until tender, about 3 minutes.
4. Blend together cornstarch, bouillon, and soy sauce. Stir into mixture and cook, stirring constantly, until smooth and mixture comes to a boil.
5. Serve immediately with hot cooked rice and additional soy sauce.
6. Makes 6 servings.

RANCHER SUPPER STEW

1 pound ground beef
1 envelope (1⅜ ounces) onion soup mix
2 cans (1 pound each) tomatoes
¼ cup barley
2½ cups water
2 teaspoons chili powder
2 medium carrots
1 green pepper
2 medium potatoes
½ cup sliced celery

1. Brown meat over medium-high heat in Dutch oven.
2. Add soup mix, tomatoes, barley, water and chili powder. Bring to a boil.
3. Reduce heat to low. Cover with vac-control valve closed. Cook over low heat 40 minutes.
4. Scrub carrots, and peel if necessary. Cut in thin slices.
5. Wash green pepper, split in half, remove seeds and cut in large chunks.
6. Peel potatoes and cut in pieces about 1½ inches square.
7. Add carrots, pepper, potatoes and celery to meat mixture.
8. Cover with vac-control valve closed. Cook over low heat about 20 minutes or until vegetables are tender.
9. Makes 6 to 8 servings.

CORNED BEEF AND CABBAGE

4 to 5 pounds corned beef
  Cold water
4 whole cloves
1 bay leaf
1 whole onion
2 stalks celery, sliced
1 medium-sized head cabbage

1. Place corned beef in Dutch oven. Cover with cold water. Add cloves, bay leaf, onion and celery. Bring to a boil over medium-high heat.
2. Reduce heat to low and simmer 5 minutes. With a large metal spoon, skim off fat and meat particles from top of liquid.
3. Cover tightly with vac-control valve closed. Simmer 3 to 4 hours or until corned beef is tender. Add hot water during cooking period, if it is needed.
4. Cut cabbage into wedges, remove part of center core. Place cabbage on top of meat. Cover and cook until cabbage is tender, 10 to 15 minutes.
5. Remove cabbage with a slotted spoon to drain. Remove corned beef and slice.
6. Makes 6 servings.

PORK

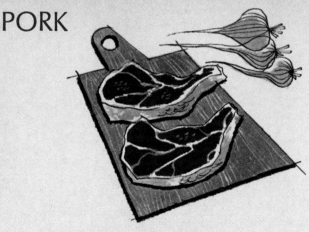

LOIN OF PORK

1. Select a loin of pork weighing 3 to 4 pounds.
2. Heat Dutch oven over medium-high heat until a piece of butcher's paper or white paper placed in bottom of pan starts to turn brown. Remove paper.
3. Place pork fat side down in pan and brown well. When the cold pork hits the hot pan it will stick, but as the meat browns and fat is released from the pork, it will loosen.
4. Turn meat and brown all sides.
5. Turn meat fat side up and season with salt and pepper. Cover and reduce heat to medium.
6. Cover with vac-control valve closed.
7. When cover is hot to the touch, in approximately 3 to 5 minutes, reduce heat to low. Roast loin of pork approximately 30 to 35 minutes per pound.

ORANGE GINGER PORK CHOPS

  6 lean pork chops
  ¼ cup orange juice
  ½ teaspoon salt
  1 teaspoon ground ginger
  6 orange slices (1 large orange)
  ¾ cup dairy sour cream

1. Heat skillet over medium-high heat. Place pork chops in skillet and brown well on both sides. Pork chops will loosen from pan as they brown and fat cooks out of meat.
2. Add orange juice.
3. Reduce heat to low and cover with vac-control closed. Simmer about 30 minutes.
4. Uncover and sprinkle chops with salt and ginger and top each with an orange slice. Cover and simmer 10 to 15 minutes or until chops are fork tender.
5. Remove chops to an oven-proof platter and top each chop with a tablespoon of sour cream. Place under broiler, about 3 inches from source of heat, and broil 1 minute. Serve immediately.
6. Makes 6 servings.

DIXIE PORK CHOPS

  6 loin or rib pork chops 1 inch thick
    Salt and pepper
  2 cups tomato juice
  1½ tablespoons Worcestershire sauce
  1 teaspoon lemon juice
  ¼ cup chopped green pepper
  ¼ cup chopped onion

1. Place pork chops in cold large skillet. Place over medium heat and brown chops thorroughly on both sides.
2. Season with salt and pepper.
3. Combine remaining ingredients and pour over chops.
4. Cover with vac-control valve closed and cook over low heat 1 hour or until chops are very tender.
5. Serve with hot cooked rice or whipped potatoes.
6. Makes 6 servings.

STUFFED PORK CHOPS

  4 pork chops, 1- to 1½-inches thick
  1 cup coarse dry bread crumbs
  ¾ cup chopped apples
  3 tablespoons chopped raisins
  ½ teaspoon salt
  2 tablespoons sugar
  2 tablespoons minced onion
    Dash pepper
    Dash sage
  2 tablespoons melted butter or margarine
    Water
    Flour
  1 tablespoon shortening

1. Have butcher cut a pocket in each pork chop.
2. Combine bread crumbs, apples, raisins, salt, sugar, onion, pepper, sage, and melted butter. Toss together lightly. Moisten slightly with a little water if stuffing is dry.
3. Fill pockets in pork chops with the mixture. Fasten openings together with toothpicks or skewers.
4. Dust pork chops lightly with flour. Melt fat in skillet over medium high heat. Place pork chops in skillet and brown well on both sides.
5. Add ¼ cup water.
6. Cover skillet with vac-control valve closed and cook over low heat 1½ hours or until pork chops are very tender. Add water in small amounts during cooking period, if necessary. Turn chops once during cooking process.
7. Makes 4 servings.

SWEET AND PUNGENT PORK

3 large green peppers
1 pound lean pork
1 egg
2 tablespoons flour
½ teaspoon salt
    Dash of pepper
¾ cup salad oil
1 teaspoon salt
1 small clove garlic
1 cup chicken bouillon, divided
2½ tablespoons cornstarch
2 teaspoons soy sauce
½ cup vinegar
½ cup sugar
4 slices canned pineapple

1. Wash green peppers. Cut each pepper into 6 or 8 large chunks, discarding seeds and top.
2. Place green peppers in a small saucepan. Add ½ cup boiling water.
3. Cover with vac-control valve closed. Bring to a boil over medium-high heat and boil 3 minutes.
4. Drain green peppers and reserve.
5. Cut pork into ½-inch cubes.
6. Beat egg in a small bowl. Beat in flour, salt and pepper to make a batter. Add pork pieces to batter and mix lightly until every piece of pork is coated.
7. Heat salad oil and salt in skillet. Add the clove of garlic. Separate pieces of pork with a fork and drop one piece at a time into the skillet. Brown over medium heat until golden brown on one side, about 5 minutes. Turn pieces of pork over and brown on the other side. Pour off all but 1 tablespoon of the oil.
8. Pour ⅓ cup of the chicken bouillon into skillet.
9. Cover with vac-control valve closed. Reduce heat to low and simmer 10 minutes.
10. Blend together cornstarch, soy sauce, vinegar and sugar. Stir in remaining chicken bouillon to make a smooth mixture. Pour mixture into skillet. Add green pepper. Cut each pineapple slice into 6 or 8 pieces. Add to skillet.
11. Cook over medium heat, stirring constantly, until mixture comes to a boil and becomes clear and thick.
12. Serve immediately with hot cooked rice.
13. Makes 4 servings.

BAKED STUFFED SPARERIBS

4 pounds spareribs
    Salt and pepper
¼ pound diced salt pork
1 cup chopped celery
¼ cup chopped onion
1 cup diced tart apples
8 cups bread cubes
2 tablespoons sugar
2 tablespoons chopped parsley
1 teaspoon caraway seeds

1. Heat oven to 350°F.
2. Place spareribs in a baking pan. Sprinkle with salt and pepper. Bake 45 minutes.
3. While spareribs are baking, fry salt pork in a skillet over medium heat until crisp. Add celery, onion, and apples to salt pork and cook until tender, stirring occasionally.
4. Remove from heat and stir in bread cubes, sugar, parsley and caraway seeds.
5. At end of baking period, remove spareribs from oven and drain off excess fat.
6. Place bread mixture under spareribs in baking pan. Continue roasting for 1 hour or until spareribs are brown and tender.
7. Remove spareribs and cut into 1- or 2-rib serving pieces and serve over hot stuffing.
8. Makes 6 servings.

BARBECUED SPARERIBS

2 sides spareribs, about 4 pounds
½ cup catsup
1 cup water
½ teaspoon chili powder
1½ tablespoons Worcestershire sauce
2 tablespoons vinegar
1 teaspoon salt
1 tablespoon sugar
1 teaspoon dry mustard
2 onions, sliced

1. Heat oven to 325°F.
2. Cut spareribs into serving pieces.
3. Combine catsup, water, chili powder, Worcestershire sauce, vinegar, salt, sugar, and mustard.
4. Place a layer of ribs in roasting pan. Cover with sliced onions and half of the sauce. Repeat layers.
5. Cover pan with cover or foil.
6. Bake 2 hours. Uncover last half hour of cooking to brown ribs.
7. Makes 4 servings.

SAVORY PORK PIE

⅓ cup butter or margarine, divided
1 pound boned pork shoulder, cut into 1-inch cubes
4 medium onions, sliced
¼ cup flour
1 cup milk
1 can (8 ounces) tomato sauce
2 tablespoons brown sugar
1 tablespoon vinegar
1 teaspoon salt
½ teaspoon Worcestershire sauce
1 can (4 ounces) sliced mushrooms, drained
1 can (No. 2) white potatoes, drained
1 cup biscuit mix
1 teaspoon poppy seeds
⅓ cup milk

1. Heat 2 tablespoons butter in a skillet. Add pork cubes and cook in hot butter until brown on all sides.
2. Add onions to meat and cook slowly until onions are tender.
3. Remove meat and onions from skillet.
4. Melt remaining butter in skillet. Stir in flour.
5. Remove from heat and stir in milk and tomato sauce.
6. Cook over low heat, stirring constantly, until sauce thickens. Mix in brown sugar, vinegar, salt, and Worcestershire sauce.
7. Return meat and onions to skillet.
8. Cover with vac-control valve closed. Cook over low heat 45 minutes.
9. Stir mushrooms and potatoes into pork. Turn mixture into a 3-quart casserole.
10. Heat oven to 350°F.
11. Mix together biscuit mix and poppy seeds in a bowl.
12. Stir in milk to make a stiff dough.
13. Pat dough out on a lightly floured board to ½-inch thickness. With a floured biscuit cutter, cut into 1½-inch circles. Place circles on top of meat mixture in casserole.
14. Bake 30 minutes or until biscuits are light golden brown.
15. Makes 4 to 6 servings.

PAN-BROILED BACON

1. Place several slices of bacon in a cold skillet. Do not separate slices, they will separate as they get warm and cook.
2. Place over low heat.
3. As bacon cooks, separate slices and turn frequently. Drain off excess fat during browning.
4. Cook to desired degree of crispness. Drain on paper toweling.

BAKED HAM

4 pounds ready-to-eat-ham, butt end
2 tablespoons prepared mustard
¼ cup brown sugar
Whole cloves

1. Heat Dutch oven over medium-high heat until a piece of butcher's paper or white paper placed in bottom of pan starts to turn brown. Remove paper.
2. Add ham and brown well on all sides. Turn fat side up.
3. Cover with vac-control valve closed, or for larger hams use dome cover. Reduce heat to low and cook 30 minutes.
4. Remove Dutch oven from heat. Spread top of ham with prepared mustard. Pat brown sugar over top of ham. Insert cloves over surface of ham.
5. Cover and cook over low heat 30 minutes longer.
6. Makes 6 to 8 servings.

PORK IN ORANGE-MUSTARD SAUCE

4 pound roast loin of pork, boned and rolled
Salt
Freshly ground black pepper
4 cloves garlic, minced
1 onion, quartered
3 cups orange juice
3 tablespoons prepared mustard

1. Preheat Dutch oven over medium-high heat. Put pork in Dutch oven and brown well on all sides.
2. Sprinkle with salt and pepper. Add garlic and onion and continue browning for a few minutes, until onion is lightly browned.
3. Add orange juice and mustard.
4. Cover with vac-control valve closed and simmer over low heat 1½ to 2 hours or until pork is tender. Let pork cool in Dutch oven.
5. Refrigerate pork several hours or overnight in juices.
6. Remove fat and strain juices.
7. Heat oven to 325°F.
8. Slice pork in ½-inch thick slices and arrange in a shallow casserole. Cover with sauce. Cover casserole.
9. Heat in oven about 30 minutes or until thoroughly heated. Serve with rice.
10. Makes 6 to 8 servings.

LAMB

ROAST LEG OF LAMB

1. For a small roast select either the sirloin half of leg, shank half of leg or leg with sirloin off. Have butcher prepare leg of lamb for roasting.
2. If desired, rub leg of lamb with a cut clove of garlic before roasting.
3. Heat Dutch oven over medium-high heat until a piece of butcher's paper or white paper placed in bottom of pan starts to turn brown. Remove paper.
4. Place meat in Dutch oven and brown well on all sides, turning as it browns and meat loosens.
5. Reduce heat to medium and cover with vac-control valve open. Allow vapor to escape in a steady stream from vac-control valve.
6. Close vac-control valve and reduce heat to low. Roast 30 to 35 minutes per pound. If you like a touch of pink in your roast lamb, cut cooking time down to about 25 minutes per pound.
7. Turn roast and season with salt and pepper near end of cooking period.
8. Leg of lamb is nice served with mint sauce.

SHERRIED LAMB CHOPS

4 shoulder lamb chops
  Salt and pepper
¼ cup salad oil
1 clove garlic
½ cup dry sherry
½ cup hot water
1 bouillon cube
8 small white onions, peeled
6 carrots, peeled and cut in small chunks
4 small potatoes, peeled and halved

1. Sprinkle chops on both sides with salt and pepper.
2. Heat oil in large skillet over medium heat.
3. Add garlic and lamb chops. Brown chops on both sides.
4. Remove garlic.
5. Add sherry, hot water and bouillon cube.
6. Cover, with vac-control valve closed. Cook over low heat about 25 minutes.
7. Place onions, carrots and potatoes around chops. Sprinkle lightly with salt and pepper.
8. Cover and simmer about 30 minutes or until vegetables are tender.
9. Makes 4 servings.

PERUVIAN LAMB CHOPS

3 tablespoons flour
1 teaspoon salt
¼ teaspoon pepper
½ teaspoon oregano
4 shoulder lamb chops, ¾-inch thick
¼ cup salad oil
¼ cup chopped green onions
¼ cup strong coffee
¼ cup dairy sour cream
¼ cup grated Swiss cheese

1. Heat oven to 350°F.
2. Combine flour, salt, pepper and oregano. Mix well.
3. Pound flour mixture into lamb chops with the edge of a saucer.
4. Heat oil in large skillet over medium heat.
5. Add lamb chops and scallions and cook until chops are browned on both sides.
6. Arrange chops and scallions in a greased shallow casserole.
7. Combine coffee and sour cream and blend well.
8. Pour over lamb chops. Sprinkle with cheese.
9. Bake in oven 30 minutes or until tender.
10. Makes 4 servings.

LAMB SHOULDER CHOP AND LEEKS

6 shoulder lamb chops, 1 inch thick
1 can (10¾ ounces) condensed tomato rice soup
½ cup water
½ teaspoon salt
¼ teaspoon caraway seeds
⅛ teaspoon black pepper
1 bunch leeks, trimmed and halved lengthwise

1. Place skillet over medium-high heat. Place a small square of butcher's paper or white paper in bottom of pan. When paper turns brown the skillet is ready for use. Remove paper.
2. Place lamb chops in skillet and brown well on both sides. Drain off lamb fat drippings.
3. Combine soup, water, salt, caraway seeds and pepper. Pour over lamb chops. Cover skillet with the vac-control valve closed, lower heat, and simmer 15 minutes.
4. Add leeks to skillet. Cover tightly and simmer 30 minutes longer.
5. Serve with hot cooked rice, if desired.
6. Makes 6 servings.

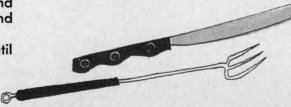

BRAISED LAMB SHANKS WITH VEGETABLES

4 lamb shanks
1 clove garlic
¼ cup flour
2 teaspoons salt
¼ teaspoon pepper
3 tablespoons salad oil
1 onion, sliced
½ cup catsup
1 bottle or can (12 ounces) beer or ale
8 pared carrots, quartered
8 small whole white onions, peeled
4 potatoes, peeled and cut into chunks

1. Trim any extra fat from lamb shanks. Rub well with cut garlic clove.
2. Combine flour, salt and pepper. Roll lamb shanks in this mixture to coat evenly.
3. Heat oil in Dutch oven over medium-high heat.
4. Add lamb shanks and brown well on all sides.
5. Add onion, catsup and beer or ale.
6. Cover, with vac-control valve open. Reduce heat to medium and allow vapor to escape in a steady stream.
7. Close vac-control valve in cover and reduce heat to low.
8. Cook over low heat about 1½ hours or until lamb is almost tender.
9. Add vegetables and cook about 30 minutes longer or until meat and vegetables are tender.
10. Makes 4 servings.

LAMB CASSEROLE

1 tablespoon salad oil
1 pound shoulder lamb, cut into 1½-inch cubes
¼ cup flour
1¼ teaspoons salt
⅛ teaspoon pepper
¼ teaspoon rosemary
1½ cups beef bouillon
¾ cup chopped celery
¾ cup diced potatoes
½ cup thinly sliced carrots
¼ cup chopped green pepper
½ cup sliced onions

1. Heat oven to 350°F.
2. Heat oil in skillet over medium heat. Add lamb and cook, stirring occasionally, until browned on all sides. Remove lamb with a slotted spoon.
3. Add flour, salt, pepper, and rosemary to remaining fat in skillet. Stir in bouillon and cook, stirring constantly, until mixture comes to a boil and is thickened. Add lamb and remaining ingredients and blend well.
4. Turn mixture into a 1½ quart casserole. Cover and bake 1½ hours or until lamb and vegetables are tender.
5. Makes 4 servings.

LAMB STEW

2 pounds lamb neck slices
2 tablespoons flour
2 tablespoons salad oil
1 medium onion, sliced
½ cup sliced celery
1 can (1 pound, 3 ounces) tomatoes
4 whole cloves
1 bay leaf
2 teaspoons salt
½ teaspoon Ac'cent
¼ teaspoon pepper
1 cup water
4 small potatoes, cubed
4 medium carrots, sliced

1. Coat lamb slices with flour.
2. Heat oil in Dutch oven over medium-high heat. Add lamb slices and brown well on all sides. Remove lamb and reserve.
3. Add onion and celery to Dutch oven and brown lightly. Remove and reserve. Discard excess oil in Dutch oven.
4. Return lamb to Dutch oven. Add tomatoes, cloves, bay leaf, salt, Ac'cent, and pepper. Add water. Bring to a boil. Reduce heat. Cover and simmer about 45 minutes, stirring occasionally.
5. Return onion and celery to lamb. Add potatoes and carrots. Cover and simmer 15 minutes. Remove cover and simmer 15 minutes or until meat and vegetables are tender.
6. Makes 4 servings.

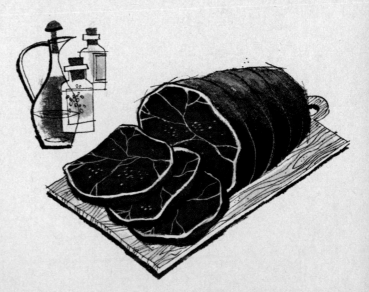

LAMB CHILINDRON

3 tablespoons olive oil
1½ pounds lamb, cut in cubes
1 teaspoon paprika
1 large onion, chopped
2 garlic cloves, crushed
1 can (5 ounces) pimientos, drained and chopped
1 bay leaf, crumbled
1½ teaspoons salt
1 can (1 pound) tomatoes
½ cup dry red wine
2 slices stale bread
Olive oil

1. Heat olive oil in Dutch oven over medium heat.
2. Add lamb cubes and brown well on all sides.
3. Add paprika, onions, garlic and pimiento.
4. Turn heat to low and cook until onions are soft.
5. Add bay leaf, salt, tomatoes and wine.
6. Cover with vac-control valve closed. Cook over low heat about 1½ hours or until meat is tender.
7. Cut stale bread into small cubes.
8. Fry cubes in hot olive oil in skillet until golden brown on all sides. Drain well on absorbent paper.
9. Add bread cubes to stew during last 10 minutes of cooking.
10. Makes 4 to 6 servings.

LAMB-STUFFED PEPPERS

4 medium green peppers
Boiling water
1 pound ground lamb
1 egg, beaten
⅓ cup sweet pickle relish
1 small onion, finely chopped
2 tablespoons dry bread crumbs
½ cup milk
¾ teaspoon salt
½ teaspoon oregano
⅛ teaspoon pepper
1 can (8 ounces) tomato sauce with cheese

1. Heat oven to 350°F.
2. Cut green peppers in half lengthwise. Remove seeds and white membrane. Place green peppers in a saucepan. Cover peppers with boiling water, place over high heat and boil for 1 minute. Drain thoroughly.
3. Combine lamb, egg, pickle relish, onion, bread crumbs, milk, salt, oregano and pepper. Mix together lightly. Fill pepper halves with lamb mixture.

4. Place stuffed pepper halves in a shallow baking dish.
5. Bake about 25 minutes or until thoroughly heated.
6. Put tomato sauce in a small saucepan and heat thoroughly. Serve with stuffed green peppers.
7. Makes 4 servings.

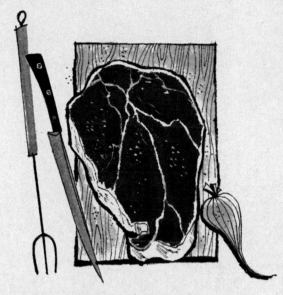

ITALIAN LAMB AND BEAN STEW

2 pounds lamb neck slices
2 tablespoons salad oil
1 small onion, sliced
1 clove garlic, minced
1 can (1 pound, 4 ounces) tomatoes
1½ teaspoons salt
¼ teaspoon oregano
⅛ teaspoon pepper
1 or 2 small bay leaves
¼ pound small fresh mushrooms, washed
2 medium zucchini, cut in ½-inch thick slices
2 cans (1 pound, 4 ounces each) white kidney beans, drained
½ cup pitted ripe olives, halved

1. In a Dutch oven, over medium-high heat, brown lamb in hot salad oil. When lamb is browned, pour off all drippings.
2. Add onion, garlic, tomatoes, salt, oregano, pepper, and bay leaf. Cover and simmer over low heat 45 minutes.
3. Remove bay leaf. Add mushrooms and zucchini. Cover and simmer 15 minutes longer or until vegetables and lamb are tender.
4. Add kidney beans and olives. Simmer uncovered for about 5 minutes, or until beans are hot.
6. Serve with crusty Italian bread to mop up the gravy.
7. Makes 4 to 6 servings.

IRISH LAMB STEW

2 pounds boned shoulder of lamb, cut in 2-inch pieces
1 quart water
2 sprigs parsley
1 bay leaf
2 celery tops
2 teaspoons salt
2 teaspoons Ac'cent
2 cups cubed yellow turnips
6 small onions, peeled
3 medium potatoes, pared and halved
2 tablespoons flour
3 tablespoons water

1. Put lamb in a saucepan or Dutch oven with water, parsley, bay leaf, celery tops, salt and Ac'cent. Cover and simmer 1½ hours or until lamb is tender.
2. Add turnips, onions and potatoes. Cover and cook until vegetables are tender.
3. Combine flour and water and stir until smooth. Stir into lamb mixture and cook, stirring constantly, until broth is thickened.
4. Makes 6 servings.

LAMB COTTAGE PIE

2 tablespoons butter or margarine
½ cup chopped celery
½ cup chopped onion
1 medium tomato, peeled and chopped
½ cup chicken bouillon
1 teaspoon salt
½ teaspoon oregano
½ teaspoon sage
⅛ teaspoon pepper
1 teaspoon Worcestershire sauce
4 cups minced cooked lamb
1 envelope instant mashed potato
¾ cup grated Cheddar cheese

1. Heat oven to 400°F.
2. Heat butter in a large skillet over medium-high heat.
3. When butter is hot, cook celery and onion just until crisply tender, but not browned.
4. Add tomato, bouillon, salt, oregano, sage, pepper, Worcestershire sauce, and lamb. Remove from heat and pour mixture into a 2-quart casserole.
5. Prepare instant mashed potatoes according to directions on package. Stir in ½ cup of the grated cheese.
6. Spoon potatoes over meat mixture in casserole. Sprinkle remaining cheese over top of potato layer.
7. Bake 30 minutes or until mixture is piping hot and top is lightly browned.
8. Makes 4 to 6 servings.

LAMB SHANKS

4 lamb shanks
¼ cup flour
½ teaspoon salt
Dash of pepper
¼ cup salad oil
½ cup chopped onion
1 clove garlic, minced
½ cup chopped celery
1 can (8-ounces) tomato sauce
½ cup dry red table wine
1 bay leaf

1. Dredge lamb shanks in flour mixed with salt and pepper.
2. Heat salad oil in skillet over medium heat. Add lamb shanks and brown well on all sides.
3. Add onion, garlic, celery, tomato sauce, wine and bay leaf. Cover with vac-control valve closed. Lower heat and simmer 1½ to 2 hours or until meat is very tender. Turn and baste lamb shanks occasionally during cooking time. Add a little more wine if gravy gets too thick.
4. Before serving add additional salt and pepper if needed.
5. Makes 4 servings.

BRAISED SHOULDER OF LAMB

¼ cup flour
½ teaspoon salt
Dash of pepper
4 to 5 pounds lamb shoulder, boned and rolled
2 tablespoons butter or margarine
1 large onion, chopped
1 clove garlic, minced
1 cup dry red table wine
1 cup hot water
1 bay leaf
3 pepper corns
Pinch of thyme

1. Combine flour, salt and pepper. Dredge lamb roast with flour mixture.
2. Melt butter in Dutch oven medium heat. Add lamb and brown well on all sides.
3. Add onion, garlic, wine, water, bay leaf, peppercorns, thyme and salt to taste. Cover with vac-control valve closed. Lower heat and simmer 2 to 2½ hours or until meat is tender. Turn meat occasionally during cooking time.
4. Cut lamb in slices for serving. Strain juices in pan and serve with lamb.
5. Makes 6 to 8 servings.

VEAL

VEAL CUTLETS, ORIENTAL

4 veal cutlets
Flour
3 tablespoons fat
½ cup chopped celery
¼ cup chopped onion
½ cup sliced mushrooms
3 tablespoons soy sauce
1 chicken bouillon cube
1 cup hot water
1 tablespoon cornstarch
½ cup slivered almonds, toasted
Hot cooked rice

1. Dip veal cutlets in flour.
2. Heat fat in a skillet over medium high-heat. Brown veal until lightly browned on both sides. Remove veal.
3. Add celery, onion and mushrooms to pan. Cook until limp but not browned. Return veal to pan.
4. Add soy sauce. Dissolve bouillon cube in hot water. Add ½ cup bouillon to skillet. Turn heat to low. Cover and simmer 30 minutes.
5. Combine remaining ½ cup bouillon and cornstarch. Stir into veal mixture. Cook, stirring constantly, until clear and thickened. Stir in almonds.
6. Serve over hot cooked rice.
7. Makes 4 servings.

PARTY VEAL POT ROAST

6 pound boned veal rump roast
1 pint dairy sour cream
1 package (1⅜ ounces) onion soup mix
¼ cup finely snipped fresh dill or 2 teaspoons dill seeds
1 teaspoon salt
¼ teaspoon freshly ground black pepper

1. Pre-heat Dutch oven over medium-high heat. Add veal roast and brown well on all sides. It will sizzle and spit as it browns if the heat is right.
2. Combine sour cream and onion soup mix. Spread over top of veal roast. Add dill, salt and pepper.
3. Cover with vac-control valve closed. Lower heat and simmer 2½ to 3 hours or until veal is tender.
4. Remove roast to heated serving platter. Serve with hot buttered noodles and gravy.
5. Makes 8 to 10 servings.

BRAISED SHOULDER OF VEAL

4 pounds veal shoulder
2 cloves garlic
1 teaspoon salt
1 teaspoon freshly ground pepper
1 cup bouillon
1 cup dry white wine
1 teaspoon tarragon
1 onion
½ bay leaf

1. Have butcher bone, roll and tie veal shoulder. Be sure to take the bones also.
2. Make small incisions in the meat with a sharp knife and insert thin slivers of garlic.
3. Pre-heat Dutch oven over medium-high heat. Add veal and brown very well on all sides, turning often. It will sizzle and spit as it cooks if the heat is right, to get a good brown color.
4. Sprinkle with salt and pepper. Add bouillon, white wine, tarragon, onion and bay leaf. Add the veal bones.
5. Cover with vac-control valve closed. Lower heat and simmer gently about 2 hours or until veal is tender.
6. Remove veal to a hot serving platter. Remove strings and slice. Skim fat from juices in the pan. Remove onion, bay leaf and bones. Serve sauce with veal.
7. Makes 4 to 6 servings.

VEAL CHOPS ALL-IN-ONE

4 veal chops, about ½-inch thick
2 tablespoons flour
3 tablespoons butter or margarine
⅓ cup grated Parmesan cheese
1 teaspoon salt
¼ teaspoon pepper
4 cups thinly sliced potatoes
2 cups thinly sliced onions
3 beef bouillon cubes
¾ cup hot water
1 tablespoon lemon juice

1. Coat veal chops with flour.
2. Melt butter in skillet over medium heat. Brown veal chops well on both sides.
3. Combine cheese, salt and pepper. Sprinkle 2 tablespoons of mixture over chops. Cover with potatoes. Sprinkle with 2 tablespoons more of cheese mixture. Cover with onion slices and remaining cheese.
4. Dissolve bouillon cubes in hot water. Add lemon juice and pour over onions in skillet.
5. Cover with vac-control valve closed. Lower heat and simmer about 40 minutes or until meat and vegetables are tender.
6. Makes 4 servings.

VEAL ITALIAN

1 pound very thin veal cutlets
4 thin slices Gruyere or Swiss cheese
4 thin slices prosciutto
  Salt
  Freshly ground black pepper
  Flour
2 tablespoons butter
3 tablespoons olive oil
½ cup dry white wine
½ cup chicken bouillon

1. Have butcher flatten veal unti it is ⅛ inch thick. Cut into 8 pieces.
2. Place a slice of cheese and a slice of prosciutto on 4 pieces of veal. Top with remaining 4 slices of veal. Press edges of veal together to seal, or fasten securely with toothpicks.
3. Season with salt and pepper. Dip in flour and shake off excess flour.
4. Melt butter and oil in a skillet over medium-high heat. When the foam subsides, add veal and cook, two at a time, turning gently, until well browned on both sides. Remove veal to a platter.
5. Discard most of fat from skillet, leaving a thin film on the bottom. Pour in wine and bouillon and bring to a boil, stirring up any browned bits of veal on bottom of pan.
6. Return veal to pan. Reduce heat, cover tightly and simmer about 20 minutes, or until veal is tender. Turn veal over once during cooking period.
7. Remove veal to a heated serving platter and pour sauce over the top.
8. Makes 4 servings.

* * * * *

VEAL AND PEPPERS

1½ pounds boneless lean veal
3 tablespoons olive oil
2 green peppers, cut into eighths
1 can (3 ounces) sliced mushrooms
2 cans (8 ounces each) tomato sauce
  Salt and pepper

1. Cut veal into bite-sized pieces.
2. Heat oil in skillet over medium-high heat. Add veal and brown on all sides.
3. Add green pepper, cover, and lower heat. Simmer 10 minutes, stirring occasionally.
4. Add mushrooms and liquid and tomato sauce. Simmer, covered, for 30 minutes or until veal is tender.
5. Season to taste with salt and pepper.
6. Makes 4 servings.

SPICY VEAL POT ROAST

1 tablespoon dry mustard
1 teaspoon poultry seasoning
1 tablespoon brown sugar
1 tablespoon salt
¼ teaspoon pepper
4 pounds veal rump or veal leg roast
3 tablespoons fat
2 tablespoons vinegar
1 onion, sliced
¼ cup water

1. Combine mustard, poultry seasoning, brown sugar, salt, pepper and flour. Rub well into veal roast.
2. Melt the fat in Dutch oven over medium-high heat. Add veal and brown well on all sides.
3. Add vinegar, onion and water.
4. Cover with vac-control valve closed and simmer over very low heat 2½ hours. Turn meat once or twice during cooking time.
5. Slice and serve with pan gravy.
6. Makes 6 to 8 servings.

BLANQUETTE OF VEAL

¼ cup butter or margarine
2 pounds boneless leg of veal, cut in 1-inch cubes
1 cup thinly sliced carrots
1 cup thinly sliced onion rings
1 teaspoon salt
¼ teaspoon thyme
1 bay leaf
2 cans (10½ ounces) condensed cream of chicken soup
1 cup light cream
2 egg yolks, beaten
2 tablespoons lemon juice

1. Heat butter in Dutch oven over medium-high heat.
2. Cook veal cubes in hot fat, stirring lightly, until golden brown on all sides.
3. Add carrots, onion rings, salt, thyme and bay leaf. Stir in chicken soup and light cream.
4. Cover with vac-control valve closed. Lower heat and simmer 45 to 60 minutes or until veal is tender.
5. Remove from heat and beat in egg yolks and lemon juice. *Heat, but do not boil.*
6. Makes 6 servings.

VEAL SCALLOPS WITH LEMON

1½ pounds veal scallops, cut ⅜ inch thick
Salt
Freshly ground black pepper
Flour
2 tablespoons butter or margarine
3 tablespoons olive oil
½ cup chicken bouillon
1 lemon, cut in thin slices

1. Place scallops between 2 pieces of waxed paper. Pound flat with the side of a cleaver or any heavy object. Scallops should be only ¼ inch thick.
2. Sprinkle salt and pepper on scallops. Dust with flour and shake off any excess.
3. Melt butter and oil in skillet over medium heat. Add veal scallops, a few at a time, and cook about 2 minutes on each side or until they are golden brown. Remove scallops and set aside.
4. Pour off most of fat from skillet. Add chicken bouillon and boil about 1 minute scraping up any brown bits on the bottom of the skillet.
5. Return veal to skillet. Place lemon slices on top. Cover with vac-control valve closed. Lower heat and simmer 10 to 15 minutes or until veal is tender.
6. Place scallops on a heated platter and pour pan juices over top.
7. Makes 4 servings.

VEAL BIRDS

1½ pounds veal steak, cut ¼ inch thick
6 tablespoons butter or margarine, divided
2 cups soft bread crumbs
2 tablespoons minced onion
⅛ teaspoon thyme
⅛ teaspoon marjoram
½ teaspoon salt
Dash of freshly ground black pepper
Flour
½ cup dry white table wine
½ cup chicken bouillon
2 tablespoons chopped parsley

1. Pound meat with the edge of a heavy saucer or the flat side of a cleaver until very thin. Cut in six even-sized pieces.
2. Melt 4 tablespoons of the butter. Add bread crumbs, onion, thyme, marjoram, salt and pepper. Blend well.
3. Place some of the bread crumb mixture on each piece of veal. Roll up and tie with string or fasten with toothpicks. Roll birds in flour. Shake off any excess flour.

4. Melt remaining 2 tablespoons of butter in skillet over medium heat. Add birds and brown lightly on all sides.
5. Add wine, bouillon, parsley and additional salt and pepper to taste. Cover with vac-control valve closed. Lower heat and simmer gently about 45 minutes, or until meat is tender. Turn birds occasionally during cooking time.
6. Serve with pan juices.
7. Makes 6 servings.

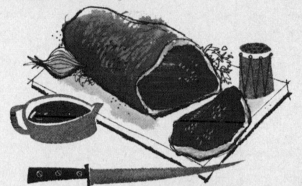

VEAL AND MUSHROOMS ON CURRIED RICE

4 tablespoons butter or margarine, divided
½ cup chopped onions
1 can (4 ounces) sliced mushrooms, drained
1 pound cubed boneless veal
Flour
1½ teaspoon salt
¼ teaspoon pepper
1½ cups water
2 beef bouillon cubes
3 cups hot cooked rice
1 teaspoon curry powder
Butter or margarine

1. Melt 2 tablespoons butter in a skillet over medium-high heat. Add onions and drained mushrooms and cook until onions are limp but not browned. Remove onions and mushrooms from skillet with a slotted spoon. Reserve.
2. Add remaining fat to skillet and heat. Dust veal with flour. Place veal in skillet and brown lightly on all sides.
3. Sprinkle with salt and pepper. Add mushrooms and onions. Add water and bouillon cubes.
4. Cover with vac-control valve closed and simmer 1 to 1½ hours, or until veal is tender.
5. Toss hot cooked rice with curry powder and several tablespoons of butter or margarine. Serve rice topped with hot cooked veal and mushrooms.
6. Makes 4 servings.

BREAST OF VEAL WITH MUSHROOM STUFFING

3½ to 4 pound breast of veal with a pocket
2 teaspoons salt
½ teaspoon freshly ground black pepper
4 tablespoons butter, divided
½ cup chopped onions
¼ pound mushrooms, sliced
1 cup fresh bread crumbs
¼ cup sour cream
1 egg, beaten
1 tablespoon minced parsley
1 cup dry white wine
½ cup water
1 carrot, sliced
1 onion, sliced

1. Rub veal with 1 teaspoon salt and ¼ teaspoon black pepper.
2. Melt 2 tablespoons butter in a skillet. Add onions and mushrooms and cook until onions are limp but not browned.
3. Turn mixture into a bowl. Add bread crumbs, sour cream, egg and parsley. Mix in remaining salt and pepper.
4. Stuff pocket in veal with mixture. Sew or skewer opening together.
5. Melt remaining butter in Dutch oven. Add veal and brown well on all sides, turning carefully so stuffing will stay in pocket.
6. Add wine, water, carrot and onion.
7. Cover with vac-control valve closed and cook over low heat 2 to 2½ hours or until veal is tender.
8. Place veal on warm serving platter. Remove cords or skewers. Strain gravy and serve with veal.
9. Makes about 6 to 8 servings.

VEAL PARMIGIANO

1 pound thin veal cutlets
   Olive or salad oil
3 cloves garlic, finely minced
1 onion, minced
1 can (1 pound 4 ounces) tomatoes
1¼ teaspoons salt
   Dash of pepper
1 can (8 ounces) tomato sauce
¼ teaspoon oregano
1 egg
¼ cup packaged dried bread crumbs
½ cup grated Parmesan cheese, divided
½ pound Mozzarella cheese

1. Have butcher cut veal into 8 pieces, about 4½ by 2 inches in size.
2. Heat 3 tablespoons of olive oil in a saucepan over medium heat. Add garlic and onion and cook until lightly browned. Add tomatoes, salt, pepper, tomato sauce and oregano. Do not cover. Simmer about 30 minutes, stirring occasionally to break up tomatoes.
3. Beat egg lightly with a fork. Combine crumbs and ¼ cup Parmesan cheese on a piece of waxed paper. Dip each piece of veal in the beaten egg, then into the crumbs.
4. Heat 1 tablespoon olive oil in a skillet over medium-high heat. Add 3 pieces of the veal and cook until golden brown on both sides. Repeat process, using remaining 2 tablespoons of olive oil and cooking the rest of the veal. Place browned pieces of veal in a 12 by 8 by 2 inch baking pan.
5. Heat oven to 350°F.
6. Cut Mozzarella cheese into very thin slices. Pour about two-thirds of the tomato sauce over veal in baking pan. Cover with slices of Mozzarella cheese. Top with remaining tomato sauce. Sprinkle remaining Parmesan cheese over the top.
7. Bake, uncovered, 30 minutes or until piping hot.
8. Makes 4 generous servings.

RICE-STUFFED VEAL ROLLS

1 pound thinly sliced veal cutlet
1 cup cooked rice
2 tablespoons butter or margarine, softened
2 tablespoons chopped parsley
2 tablespoons shortening
2 tablespoons chopped onion
1 can (10¾ ounces) condensed tomato rice soup
¼ cup water
⅛ teaspoon oregano

1. Place veal cutlet between two pieces of waxed paper. Pound as thin as possible with the flat side of a cleaver or the bottom of a heavy saucepan. Cut veal into 8 pieces.
2. Combine rice, butter and parsley. Place a small amount of the mixture on each piece of veal. Roll up and fasten with toothpicks.
3. Heat shortening in skillet over medium-high heat. Add veal rolls and brown well on all sides. Pour off drippings.
4. Combine remaining ingredients and pour over veal.
5. Cover with vac-control valve closed, and cook over low heat 45 minutes. Stir and baste occasionally.
6. Makes 4 servings.

VEAL SCALLOPS, MARSALA

1½ pound thin veal scallops
Flour
3 tablespoons butter or margarine
3 tablespoons salad oil
Salt and pepper
Marsala wine
¼ cup chopped parsley

1. Ask butcher to pound scallops paper thin. If butcher doesn't pound them thin enough, do it at home. Place each scallop between 2 pieces of waxed paper and pound with the flat side of a cleaver or use a meat pounder or any heavy flat object.
2. Dust scallops with flour. Melt butter in large skillet, add oil and heat. Brown scallops quickly.
3. Cover with wine and continue cooking until the wine is reduced to half. Turn scallops once during cooking.
4. When wine is reduced and the meat is tender, remove meat to hot platter and add ¼ cup wine to the pan.
5. Bring to a boil, add parsley and pour over the veal.
6. Serve with hot cooked rice, if desired.
7. Makes 4 servings.

VEAL STEW

2½ pounds veal shoulder
2 tablespoons flour
1 teaspoon salt
½ teaspoon freshly ground black pepper
¼ cup olive or salad oil
1 teaspoon paprika
½ cup chopped green onions
1 teaspoon rosemary
1 cup dry white wine or vermouth
½ cup water
12 small onions, peeled
3 carrots, sliced

1. Ask the butcher to bone the shoulder and cut the meat into 2-inch cubes.
2. Combine flour, salt and pepper. Dredge veal cubes in flour mixture.
3. Heat oil in skillet over medium-high heat. Add veal cubes and brown well on all sides. Sprinkle veal cubes with paprika as they cook.
4. Add chopped onion, rosemary, wine and water.
5. Cover skillet with vac-control valve closed. Lower heat and simmer about 40 minutes. Add onions and carrots. Cover and simmer until vegetables are tender and meat is cooked.

6. Serve with hot buttered noodles if desired.
7. Makes 4 servings.

VEAL STEW WITH DUMPLINGS

1¼ pounds boneless veal stew meat, cut into
1-inch cubes
Flour
3 tablespoons salad oil
1 medium onion, chopped
1 envelope (1⅝ ounces) Swiss style chicken noodle soup mix
2 cups water
⅛ teaspoon rosemary
1 cup sifted flour
1½ teaspoons baking powder
½ teaspoon salt
½ cup milk
2 tablespoons salad oil

1. Coat veal cubes lightly with flour. Shake off excess flour.
2. Heat salad oil in a skillet over medium-high heat. Add veal and cook, turning often, until browned on all sides. Add onion and continue cooking for 5 minutes.
3. Add soup mix, water and rosemary.
4. Cover with vac-control valve closed and simmer 1 hour, stirring occasionally.
5. Sift together flour, baking powder and salt into a mixing bowl. Combine milk and salad oil. Stir liquid into dry ingredients and mix just enough to form a soft dough.
6. Drop dumpling mixture by tablespoonfuls on top of veal stew in skillet. Cover tightly and simmer 10 minutes. Remove cover and continue cooking until dumplings are done.
7. Serve stew and dumplings immediately.
8. Makes 4 servings.

SAUTÉED CALF'S LIVER

4 slices calf's liver, cut ⅜ inch thick
Salt and pepper
¼ cup flour
2 tablespoons butter or margarine
2 tablespoons salad oil

1. Have butcher remove filament from slices of liver.
2. Season with salt and pepper. Roll in flour and shake off excess flour.
3. Heat butter and oil in skillet over medium high heat until very hot. Place liver in skillet and cook 2 to 3 minutes. Turn liver and cook 2 to 3 minutes on second side.
4. Liver is done when it's juices run a very pale pink if a slice is pricked with a fork.
5. Serve hot with fried onions if desired.
6. Makes 4 servings.

Poultry

Poultry is probably the most versatile meat of all. It can be roasted whole or in pieces, fried, broiled, steamed, or boiled. Excellent plain, it takes on party glamour with the addition of a sauce or special seasoning. Learn a few basic recipes, then experiment with new flavors and seasonings on your own.

ROAST CHICKEN

1. Select a roasting chicken weighing 4 to 5 pounds.
2. Remove gizzard, neck, heart and liver from body cavity and use for making stock. Clean chicken and rinse with cool water. Drain and pat dry inside and out with paper toweling.
3. Stuff neck cavity lightly. Pull excess skin over opening and secure to back with skewers.
4. Fill body cavity with stuffing. Do not pack too tightly as stuffing swells during cooking. Skewer body opening and lace closed with string. Tie legs together tightly.
5. Twist wings back and tuck under shoulders to hold wings close to body, or skewer in place and tie with heavy string.
6. Spread chicken with softened butter or margarine.
7. Heat Dutch oven over medium heat until a piece of white paper placed in bottom of pan starts to turn brown. Remove paper.
8. Place chicken in pan and brown well on all sides. Season with salt and pepper.
9. Cover with vac-control valve closed. Reduce heat to low.
10. Roast chicken 20 to 25 minutes per pound or until thigh is tender. Turn chicken several times during roasting time.

BUTTER CHICKEN STUFFING

1 cup hot water
½ cup butter or margarine
¼ cup chopped onion
1 tablespoon poultry seasoning
2 teaspoons dry mustard
1 tablespoon chopped parsley
3 quarts soft bread crumbs

1. Combine water, butter, and onion in a saucepan. Bring to a boil and simmer over low heat 5 minutes. Add poultry seasoning, mustard, and parsley. Remove from heat.
2. Put bread crumbs in a mixing bowl. Pour liquid over top and toss together to blend.
3. Makes enough stuffing for a 5 pound chicken.

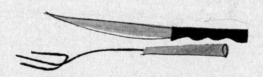

NEW PAN-FRIED CHICKEN

1 broiler-fryer chicken, cut in serving pieces
½ cup flour
2 teaspoons salt
¼ teaspoon paprika
¼ teaspoon pepper
½ teaspoon onion salt
½ cup salad oil

1. Place chicken pieces in a paper bag. Add flour, salt, paprika, pepper, and onion salt. Shake well until all pieces of chicken are evenly covered with the mixture.
2. Put salad oil in skillet and place over medium heat.
3. When oil is hot, place chicken pieces in skillet skin side down. Cover skillet with vac-control valve closed.
4. Cook over medium heat 25 minutes. Turn chicken pieces over. Cover skillet and continue cooking 20 minutes or until chicken pieces are crisply brown on the outside and tender on the inside.
5. Remove chicken pieces from pan, drain on paper toweling for 1 minute. Serve.
6. Makes 4 servings.

CHICKEN STROGANOFF

3 whole broiler-fryer chicken breasts
¼ cup butter or margarine
1½ teaspoons salt
1 medium onion, chopped
½ pound mushrooms, sliced
¼ cup dry sherry or water
½ teaspoon thyme
1 tablespoon cornstarch
1 cup sour cream
1½ teaspoons paprika

1. Have butcher bone chicken breasts. Remove skin. Cut each breast half into 10 or 12 strips.
2. Melt butter in skillet over medium-high heat. Add strips of chicken. Sprinkle with salt. Cook, stirring constantly, 3 minutes. Add onion and mushrooms and cook 2 minutes longer, continuing to stir.
3. Add sherry and thyme. Cover with vac-control valve closed. Reduce heat to medium and cook 4 minutes.
4. Blend together cornstarch and 2 tablespoons cold water. Add to skillet all at once and cook, stirring rapidly, until mixture is smooth and thickened.
5. Stir in sour cream and paprika. Heat thoroughly but do not boil.
6. Makes 6 servings.

CHICKEN A LA VALLEE D'AUGE

4 whole broiler-fryer chicken breasts
¼ cup butter or margarine
1 teaspoon salt
⅛ teaspoon pepper
2 small onions, minced
1 tablespoon chopped parsley
¼ teaspoon thyme
¼ teaspoon rosemary
¾ cup apple cider
½ cup heavy cream

1. Have butcher cut breasts in half and remove heavy breast bone.
2. Melt butter in skillet over medium-low heat. Add chicken breasts and brown slowly on all sides, about 20 minutes.
3. Add salt, pepper, onions, parsley, thyme, rosemary, and apple cider. Cover with vac-control valve closed and simmer 20 to 25 minutes or until chicken breasts are tender.
4. Remove chicken breasts to a heated serving platter. Add heavy cream to liquid in skillet. Stir and heat, but *do not boil.* Serve sauce over chicken.
5. Makes 8 servings.

CHICKEN CHOP SUEY

2 whole broiler-fryer chicken breasts
¼ cup salad oil
1 teaspoon salt
½ cup chicken bouillon
1 can (6 ounces) sliced mushrooms
2 cups diagonally sliced celery
2 tablespoons cornstarch
1 tablespoon soy sauce
⅓ cup cold water
½ cup toasted slivered almonds
¼ cup sliced green onions
Hot cooked rice

1. Have butcher bone chicken breasts. Remove skin. Cut chicken meat into ½-inch chunks.
2. Heat salad oil in skillet over medium heat. Add salt and chicken chunks and cook, stirring frequently, until lightly browned.
3. Add chicken bouillon and undrained mushrooms to chicken. Add sliced celery. Cover with vac-control valve closed. Lower heat and simmer 10 minutes or just until celery is crisply tender.
4. Meanwhile blend together cornstarch, soy sauce and cold water. Pour into liquid in skillet and cook, stirring constantly, until the liquid becomes clear and thickens and chicken mixture is very hot.
5. Arrange on a heated serving platter. Sprinkle top with slivered almonds and onions. Serve with hot cooked rice and pass soy sauce.
6. Makes 4 servings.

QUICK CHICK CREOLE

2 whole broiler-fryer chicken breasts
¼ cup butter or margarine
¼ cup chopped onion
½ teaspoon salt
¼ teaspoon pepper
2 tablespoons flour
1 can (1 pound) seasoned stewed tomatoes
¼ teaspoon Tabasco

1. Have butcher bone chicken breasts. Remove skin. Cut each breast half into 10 or 12 strips.
2. Melt butter in skillet over high heat. Add chicken and onion. Sprinkle with salt, pepper, and flour. Cook, stirring constantly, for 5 minutes.
3. Add stewed tomatoes and Tabasco. Stir. Reduce heat to medium; cover with vac-control valve closed and cook 2 minutes longer.
4. Serve over hot cooked rice.
5. Makes 4 servings.

LEMON CHICKEN

3 whole broiler-fryer chicken breasts
3 tablespoons butter or margarine
1 tablespoon flour
½ teaspoon salt
    Pinch of tarragon
1 cup chicken broth
4 lemon slices
    Chopped parsley

1. Have butcher bone chicken breasts. Remove skin and cut meat into 10 or 12 strips.
2. Melt butter in skillet over high heat. Add chicken. Sprinkle with flour, salt, and tarragon. Cook, stirring constantly, for 5 minutes.
3. Add chicken broth and lemon slices. Lower heat, cover and cook 3 minutes longer.
4. Sprinkle with chopped parsley and serve with hot cooked rice.
5. Makes 4 to 6 servings.

FRIED CHICKEN

½ cup flour
1 teaspoon Ac'cent
1 teaspoon salt
1 teaspoon paprika
⅛ teaspoon pepper
1 broiler-fryer chicken, cut in serving pieces
    Shortening or salad oil

1. Combine flour, Ac'cent, salt, paprika, and pepper. Roll chicken pieces in seasoned flour.
2. Heat shortening or salad oil, ½-inch deep, in skillet.
3. Place chicken, skin side down, in skillet. Put larger, meatier pieces in first.
4. Cook, uncovered, 15 to 25 minutes on each side, turning only once.
5. Drain well on absorbent paper.
6. Makes 4 servings.

CHICKEN TARRAGON

1 broiler-fryer chicken, cut in serving pieces
1 tablespoon seasoned salt
½ teaspoon freshly ground black pepper
    Dash of paprika
¼ cup butter or margarine
1 medium onion, thinly sliced
½ pound mushrooms, sliced
1 teaspoon tarragon

1. Sprinkle chicken pieces with combined seasoned salt, pepper, and paprika.

2. Melt butter in skillet over medium heat. When butter is hot, cook chicken to a golden brown, turning several times to brown all sides. This will take about 15 minutes.
3. Remove chicken pieces. Add onions and mushrooms to drippings in skillet and cook until onions are limp, but not browned.
4. Return chicken to skillet. Sprinkle with tarragon. Cover skillet with vac-control valve closed. Lower heat and continue cooking about 25 minutes, or until the thickest pieces of chicken are fork tender.
5. Makes about 4 servings.

CHICKEN HAWAIIAN

½ cup flour, divided
1 teaspoon salt, divided
1 broiler-fryer chicken, cut in serving pieces
½ cup shortening
⅛ teaspoon pepper
½ teaspoon ginger
2 chicken bouillon cubes
2 cups hot water
1½ cups milk
¼ cup light cream
1 can (7½ ounces) sliced mushrooms
3 cups cooked rice
1 cup canned pineapple chunks, drained

1. Heat oven to 375°F.
2. Combine ¼ cup of the flour and ½ teaspoon of the salt in a paper bag.
3. Add chicken pieces and shake well until chicken is coated with flour mixture.
4. Heat shortening in skillet over medium-high heat. Add chicken pieces and cook until golden brown on all sides.
5. Remove chicken. Stir in remaining flour, salt, pepper and ginger and mix well. Remove from heat.
6. Dissolve bouillon cubes in hot water. Stir into flour mixture in skillet. Stir in milk to make a smooth mixture.
7. Cook over medium heat, stirring constantly, until mixture is smooth and thickened. Stir in cream. Remove from heat.
8. Drain mushrooms.
9. Place cooked rice in a lightly greased 3-quart casserole. Arrange chicken pieces, mushrooms and pineapple chunks over top. Pour sauce over chicken.
10. Bake in oven 1¼ hours.
11. Makes 4 to 6 servings.

PIRATE CHICKEN CREOLE

1 broiler-fryer chicken, cut in serving pieces
1 teaspoon Ac'cent
1½ teaspoons salt, divided
½ teaspoon paprika
2 tablespoons salad oil
¼ cup water
1 medium onion, sliced
1 medium green pepper, diced
½ cup diced celery
1 can (1 pound) tomatoes
1 teaspoon dried leaf tarragon
2 tablespoons chopped parsley

1. Sprinkle chicken pieces with Ac'cent, ½ teaspoon of salt and paprika.
2. Heat salad oil in skillet over medium-high heat. Brown chicken pieces on all sides. Remove chicken from skillet.
3. Add water and bring to a boil, scraping brown particles from bottom of skillet. Add onion, green pepper, and celery. Cover with vac-control valve closed and cook 5 minutes.
4. Add remaining 1 teaspoon salt, chicken pieces, tomatoes, and tarragon. Bring to a boil. Cover tightly, with vac-control valve closed. Reduce heat and simmer 40 minutes or until chicken is tender.
5. Turn chicken into a heated serving dish and sprinkle with parsley.
6. Makes 4 servings.

CURRIED ORANGE CHICKEN

1 2½ pound broiler-fryer, cut in serving pieces
2 tablespoons butter or margarine
½ cup orange juice
1 to 2 teaspoons curry powder
2 tablespoons honey
¼ cup prepared mustard

1. Brown chicken pieces in hot fat in skillet over medium heat, until lightly browned on both sides.
2. Combine orange juice, curry powder, honey and prepared mustard. Pour over chicken in pan.
3. Cover chicken with vac-control valve closed. Cook over low heat about 45 minutes or until chicken is tender.
4. Serve chicken with hot cooked rice and orange sauce left in skillet.
5. Makes 4 servings.

CHICKEN WITH TOMATO AND AVOCADO

2 whole broiler-fryer chicken breasts
3 tablespoons butter or margarine
1 teaspoon salt
¾ cup chicken bouillon
½ teaspoon fines herbs
2 tomatoes, peeled and cut into 6 wedges each
1 avocado, peeled and diced
2 teaspoons cornstarch
Hot cooked rice

1. Have butcher bone chicken breasts. Remove skin. Cut each breast half into 10 or 12 strips. Assemble remaining ingredients.
2. Melt butter in skillet over medium-high heat. Add chicken. Sprinkle with salt. Cook 5 minutes, stirring occasionally.
3. Add chicken bouillon and herbs. Cover with vac-control valve closed. Cook 3 minutes. Add tomatoes and avocado and cook 1 minute longer.
4. Blend together cornstarch and 2 tablespoons cold water. Stir all at once into skillet. Cook, stirring rapidly, until thickened and smooth.
5. Serve immediately with hot cooked rice.
6. Makes 4 servings.

CHICKEN BREASTS WITH ALMONDS

3 whole broiler-fryer chicken breasts, boned
Salt and pepper
½ cup butter or margarine, divided
1 tablespoon minced onion
⅓ cup slivered almonds
1 teaspoon tomato paste
1 tablespoon flour
1¼ cups chicken bouillon
Pinch tarragon

1. Cut chicken breasts in half and remove skin. Sprinkle with salt and pepper.
2. Melt 6 tablespoons of the butter in a skillet. Add chicken breasts and brown slowly, Turning occasionally, for about 25 minutes. Remove chicken.
3. Add remaining 2 tablespoons butter. Add onions and almonds. Cook over low heat until almonds are browned. Blend in tomato paste and flour. Gradually add chicken bouillon and cook, stirring constantly, until mixture thickens and comes to a boil.
4. Add browned chicken to mixture in skillet. Sprinkle with a pinch of tarragon. Cover with vac-control valve closed. Lower heat and simmer 20 minutes.
5. Makes 6 servings.

CHICKEN CON LIMON

1 broiler-fryer chicken, cut in serving pieces
1 teaspoon Ac'cent
1 teaspoon salt
¼ cup butter or margarine
1 tablespoon lemon juice
1 teaspoon grated lemon rind
2 teaspoons sugar
½ cup light cream
2 tablespoons grated Parmesan cheese
1 lemon, thinly sliced

1. Sprinkle chicken pieces with Ac'cent and salt.
2. Melt butter in skillet over medium heat. Add chicken pieces and brown well on all sides. Cover with vac-control valve closed. Lower heat and cook about 30 minutes or until chicken is tender.
3. Remove chicken and place on a heat proof serving platter. Keep warm.
4. Stir lemon juice, lemon rind, and sugar into skillet. Add cream slowly and bring just to the boil, stirring constantly.
5. Pour sauce over chicken on serving platter. Sprinkle with cheese. Garnish with sliced lemon. Place in broiling compartment about 4 inches from source of heat and brown top of chicken lightly.
6. Makes 4 servings.

COUNTRY CAPTAIN CHICKEN

½ cup salad oil
2 cloves garlic, halved
2 medium onions, sliced
½ cup flour
    Salt
1 broiler-fryer chicken, cut in serving pieces
1 tablespoon curry powder
½ cup chopped celery
1 green pepper, coarsely chopped
1 can (No. 2½) tomatoes

1. Heat salad oil in skillet over medium heat. Add garlic and onion and cook until tender but not browned. Remove onion.
2. Combine flour, 1 teaspoon salt and pepper in a paper bag. Place chicken pieces in bag and shake well to coat chicken.
3. In hot oil fry chicken until golden brown on all sides. Return garlic and onions to pan. Add 2 teaspoons salt, curry powder, celery, green pepper and tomatoes.
4. Cover with vac-control valve closed. Lower heat and simmer 45 minutes or until chicken is tender.
5. Serve chicken with hot cooked rice.
6. Makes 4 servings.

CHICKEN VERONIQUE

2 broiler-fryer chickens, cut in serving pieces
2 teaspoons Ac'cent
    Salt
    Paprika
½ cup butter or margarine, divided
1 onion, finely chopped
1 clove garlic, minced
¼ pound mushrooms, sliced
4 tablespoons flour
1 teaspoon sugar
2 cups chicken bouillon
2 tablespoons lemon juice
1 cup white seedless grapes

1. Sprinkle chicken pieces with Ac'cent, salt, and paprika.
2. Melt ¼ cup of the butter in skillet over medium heat. Add chicken and brown well on all sides. Remove chicken.
3. Add remaining ¼ cup butter to the skillet. Add onion and garlic and cook over low heat 5 minutes, stirring occasionally. Add mushrooms and cook 2 minutes.
4. Blend in flour and sugar. Add bouillon and lemon juice. Cook, stirring constantly, until mixture comes to a boil and thickens.
5. Add chicken pieces. Cover with vac-control valve closed. Lower heat and simmer 30 minutes or until chicken is tender. Add grapes the last 5 minutes of cooking time.
6. Arrange chicken on a warmed serving platter and pour sauce over the top.
7. Makes 6 servings.

ROCK CORNISH GAME HENS

4 Rock Cornish hens
½ cup butter or margarine
1 cup uncooked rice
½ pound mushrooms, sliced
½ teaspoon salt
1 cup chicken bouillon
1 cup dry red table wine

1. Remove giblets from game hens. Wipe with a damp cloth. Tie legs together with string.
2. Melt butter in Dutch oven over medium heat. Put hens in Dutch oven and brown well on all sides. Remove hens and keep warm.
3. Place rice in Dutch oven and cook and stir until lightly browned. Add mushrooms, salt, bouillon and red wine. Place hens on top of mixture.
4. Cover with vac-control valve closed. Lower heat and simmer 1 hour to 1 hour and 15 minutes or until rice is cooked and hens are tender.
5. Makes 4 servings.

THAWING A FROZEN TURKEY

1. Let turkey stand in the plastic bag, partially opened, in the refrigerator for 2 to 4 days (about 24 hours for each 5 pounds); or thaw it more quickly by placing it under cold running tap water.
2. When turkey is pliable, remove giblets and neck from inside turkey. Cover with damp towel and refrigerate until ready to stuff and roast. It is best to cook it promptly, but it can be kept for 2 or 3 days under refrigeration. Never refreeze a turkey that has been thawed.

ROAST TURKEY

1. Remove thawed turkey from bag. Rinse well, especially the body cavity, and remove any bits of innards that may be left. Drain well and pat dry with paper towels.
2. Fill neck cavity lightly with stuffing, but do not pack. Fasten excess skin firmly to back of turkey with skewers.
3. Stuff body cavity lightly. Do not pack, since stuffing will expand while cooking.
4. Tuck legs under band of skin at tail or tie legs together with heavy string.
5. Tuck wings back under bird or fasten wings to body, using skewers or string.
6. Place turkey, breast side down, on a V-shaped rack in roasting pan. Roast at 325°F. according to time chart.
7. When turkey is half done, turn breast side up with protected hands.
8. Insert a meat thermometer into thickest part of thigh muscle and continue roasting until done. Thermometer should register 185°F.
9. Remove turkey to a heated platter and let stand for 20 minutes before carving.
10. While turkey is "resting," make gravy with drippings in pan and stock made from simmering giblets and neck.

Note: To roast frozen stuffed turkey, follow directions on the wrapper.

Approximate Time Chart for Roasting Turkey at 325° F.

Weight	Approximate time
6 to 8 pounds	2 to 2½ hours
8 to 12 pounds	2½ to 3½ hours
12 to 16 pounds	3½ to 4¼ hours
16 to 20 pounds	4¼ to 5 hours
20 to 24 pounds	5 to 6 hours

TURKEY GRAVY

Turkey giblets and neck
½ cup turkey fat
½ cup flour
4 cups liquid

1. Place giblets, except liver, in a saucepan. Cover with water and add a teaspoon of salt. Add a piece of onion, a celery top and a small carrot if desired.
2. Cover with vac-control valve closed and simmer over low heat 2 to 3 hours or until gizzard is fork tender. Add liver and simmer another 20 minutes. Strain broth and reserve. Cut gizzard, heart and liver into small pieces.
3. When turkey is roasted, remove to hot platter. Pour drippings from roasting pan into a bowl. Let fat rise to top of drippings and skim off into a measuring cup. Measure out ½ cup of fat and return to roasting pan. Discard remaining fat.
4. Set roasting pan over low heat and blend in flour. Cook until bubbly, stirring constantly.
5. Remove pan from heat. Combine stock from giblets and juice from roasting turkey to make 4 cups liquid. Add to fat-flour mixture in pan and stir until smooth.
6. Return to heat and cook, stirring constantly, until mixture comes to a boil and thickens. Be sure to scrape brown particles from bottom of pan while cooking. Simmer gently a few minutes and season to taste.
7. Makes 4 cups turkey gravy.

OLD FASHIONED STUFFING

4 cups diced celery
1 cup chopped onion
1 cup butter or margarine
4 quarts dry bread cubes
1 tablespoon salt
1½ teaspoons poultry seasoning
½ teaspoon sage
½ teaspoon pepper
Hot broth or water

1. Cook celery and onion in hot butter in a skillet over medium heat until onion is transparent but not browned, stirring occasionally.
2. Turn into a mixing bowl and combine with bread cubes, salt, poultry seasoning, sage, and pepper. Toss lightly.
3. If a moist dressing is preferred, add the desired amount of hot broth or water.
4. Makes enough stuffing for a 14- to 18-pound turkey.

TURKEY CURRY

¼ cup butter or margarine
¼ cup chopped onion
¼ cup flour
1 teaspoon salt
½ teaspoon ginger
1 tablespoon curry powder
2 cups milk
2 cups diced cooked turkey
¼ cup minced celery
1 cup chopped unpeeled red apple
  Hot cooked rice
  Toasted slivered almonds
  Toasted coconut
  Crisp crumbled bacon

1. Melt butter in a medium saucepan. Add onion and cook gently until onion is limp but not browned. Stir in flour, salt, ginger, and curry powder. Cook over low heat 1 minute. Remove from heat.
2. Gradually stir in milk. Return to heat and cook, stirring constantly, until mixture thickens and comes to a boil.
3. Add turkey, celery and apple. Cook over low heat, about 5 minutes, stirring occasionally.
4. Serve over hot cooked rice with toasted almonds, coconut and bacon sprinkled on top.
5. Makes 4 to 6 servings.

QUICK TURKEY DIVAN

2 packages (10 ounces) frozen asparagus
12 large slices cooked turkey
1 can (10½ ounces) condensed cream of
  chicken soup
¾ cup shredded Cheddar cheese

1. Heat oven to 375°F.
2. Cook asparagus according to basic directions in vegetable chapter. Drain and arrange pieces of asparagus in a greased shallow baking dish.
3. Cover with slices of turkey, allowing some of the green ends to show at each end of pan.
4. Pour soup over top of turkey, Sprinkle with cheese.
5. Bake 20 to 25 minutes or until hot, bubbly and lightly browned.
6. Makes 6 servings.

CORN BREAD AND SAUSAGE STUFFING

1 package (15 ounces) corn bread mix
1 pound sausage meat
3 cups chopped apples
1 cup apple juice
½ teaspoon salt

1. Prepare and bake corn bread mix according to directions on the package. Cool. Crumble coarsely into a mixing bowl.
2. Cook sausage meat in skillet over low heat. Drain on paper toweling. Cool.
3. Combine corn bread and sausage meat. Add apples, apple juice, and salt. Toss together lightly.
4. Makes enough stuffing for an 8-pound turkey.

MANDARIN DUCK

1 4 to 5 pound duckling
2 tablespoons bottled browning sauce
1 tablespoon sugar
1 teaspoon salt
1 teaspoon ginger
2 tablespoons salad oil
1 clove garlic, minced
1 cup water
½ cup sherry or orange juice
3 tablespoons cornstarch
3 tablespoons cold water

1. Cut duckling into quarters with duck shears. Place pieces in a bowl. Sprinkle with browning sauce, sugar, salt, and ginger. Stir gently to coat pieces evenly. Let stand 15 minutes.
2. Heat salad oil in Dutch oven over medium heat. Add garlic and cook a few seconds. Add pieces of duckling and cook until lightly browned on all sides. Remove duckling. Drain all fat from Dutch oven. Return duckling to Dutch oven. Add water and sherry. Cover with vac-control valve closed. Bring to a boil. Reduce heat and simmer 45 minutes or until duckling is tender.
3. Remove pieces of duckling to a warm serving platter and keep hot. Pour fat from Dutch oven, reserving as much broth as possible.
4. Combine cornstarch and cold water. Stir into broth in Dutch oven. Cook, stirring constantly, until sauce thickens and becomes clear. Taste and season to taste if necessary.
5. Serve duckling with sauce and hot cooked rice.
6. Makes 4 servings.

Shrimp Curry

Party Cooking

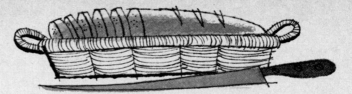

Everyone loves a party, whether it is a formal sit-down dinner or a serve-yourself buffet centered around a glamorous chafing dish. A fondue party is great fun, for your guests will cook their own food right at the table.

SHRIMP CURRY

6 tablespoons butter or margarine
1 medium onion, minced
2 stalks celery, minced
½ green pepper, minced
1 tart apple, peeled, cored and grated
2 tablespoons chopped parsley
1 to 2 tablespoons curry powder
6 tablespoons flour
3 cups chicken bouillon
½ cup cream
2 tablespoons sherry
½ teaspoon Ac'cent
2 pounds shrimp, cooked and peeled
Hot cooked rice

1. Melt butter in a saucepan over medium heat. Add onion, celery, green pepper, apple and parsley. Cook, stirring, until onion is limp but not browned.
2. Blend in curry powder and flour. Remove from heat. Stir in bouillon and cream and stir until smooth.
3. Cook over medium heat, stirring constantly, until mixture is smooth and thickened. Add sherry, Ac'cent and shrimp. Heat thoroughly.
4. Turn mixture into top part of chafing dish. Keep warm over hot water. Serve with hot cooked rice.
5. Serve with chutney, chopped onion, chopped green pepper, salted peanuts, flaked coconut and candied ginger.
6. Makes 6 servings.

ROSE'S PARTY CHICKEN

4 whole chicken breasts, split and boned
1½ teaspoon salt
¼ teaspoon pepper
1 teaspoon paprika
¾ cup butter or margarine, divided
½ pound fresh mushrooms, sliced
¼ cup flour
1⅓ cups chicken bouillon
6 tablespoons sherry
1 can (15 ounces) artichoke hearts

1. Heat oven to 350°F.
2. Sprinkle chicken breasts with salt, pepper and paprika.
3. Melt 4 tablespoons of the butter in a skillet over medium heat. Add chicken breasts and cook until lightly browned on all sides. Remove chicken breasts and place in a shallow casserole.
4. Place remaining butter in skillet. Add mushrooms and cook gently a few minutes.
5. Add flour and stir until blended. Stir in chicken bouillon and sherry. Cook over medium heat, stirring constantly, until mixture is smooth and slightly thickened. Remove from heat.
6. Drain artichoke hearts and arrange among chicken pieces. Pour sauce over top of chicken.
7. Bake 45 minutes to 1 hour or until chicken is tender.
8. Makes 4 to 6 servings.

ORANGE BLOSSOM DESSERT

2 envelopes unflavored gelatin
1½ cups cold water
1 cup sugar
2 cans (6 ounces each) frozen orange juice concentrate, kept frozen
2 cups heavy cream, whipped
Green grapes
Fresh strawberries

1. Sprinkle gelatine over cold water in a small saucepan. Place over low heat and stir until gelatine dissolves, about 4 to 5 minutes.
2. Remove from heat. Add sugar and stir until dissolved.
3. Add frozen concentrate and stir until melted. Fold in whipped cream.
4. Turn mixture into an 8-cup mold. Place in refrigerator and chill until firm.
5. Unmold onto a serving platter. Garnish with green grapes and fresh strawberries.
6. Makes 12 servings.

Orange Blossom Dessert

Rose's Party Chicken

FONDUE BOURGUIGNONNE

1 cup butter
1 cup salad oil
2½ pounds filet of beef, well trimmed and cut into ½-inch cubes

1. Place butter and oil in fondue pan. Place over medium heat and heat to 375°F.
2. Place fondue pan on stand over canned heat flame. Keep oil sizzling hot during cooking time.
3. On the table place bowls of as many different dunking sauces as desired.
4. Serve each person a plate containing raw chunks of beef. Give each person 2 forks, one two-pronged fondue fork and one regular fork. Pierce a chunk of meat with the fondue fork. Hold meat in the hot oil and brown according to taste; rare, medium, or well done will take from 10 to 30 seconds.
5. Transfer meat to regular fork, dip cooked meat into a sauce of choice and eat. Meanwhile, spear another cube of meat with fondue fork and place in hot oil.
6. Makes 6 to 8 servings.

BÉARNAISE SAUCE

2 tablespoons dry white wine
1 tablespoon tarragon vinegar
2 teaspoons dried tarragon
2 teaspoons minced shallots
½ cup butter
¼ teaspoon pepper
3 egg yolks
2 tablespoons lemon juice
¼ teaspoon salt

1. In a small saucepan combine the wine, vinegar, tarragon and shallots. Bring to a boil and cook rapidly until almost all the liquid disappears.
2. In a small saucepan heat the butter to bubbling, but do not brown.
3. In the container of an electric blender place the egg yolks, pepper, lemon juice and salt. Cover the container and flick the motor on and off at high speed.
4. Remove cover, turn motor on high and gradually add the bubbling butter. Add the herb mixture, cover and blend very quickly on high speed.
5. Makes about 1 cup sauce.

SAUCE SMITANE

¾ cup dairy sour cream
1 to 2 tablespoons grated horseradish
Salt and pepper
Chopped chives

1. Combine the sour cream with the prepared horseradish. Season to taste with salt and pepper. Add the horseradish gradually and taste often. There is a wide difference in various prepared horseradish sauces, some are mild whereas others are very strong. Sprinkle chives over top before serving.
2. Makes about ¾ cup sauce.

FONDUE CHOCOLAT

1 package (12 ounces) semi-sweet chocolate morsels
2 squares unsweetened chocolate
1 cup heavy cream
2 ounces brandy
Chunks of sponge or angel food cake
Lady fingers
Pineapple chunks, well drained
Banana chunks
Apple slices

1. Place chocolate in top part of fondue-chafer. Place water in bottom pan. Place over flame in fondue rack. Melt chocolate over the hot water. When chocolate is melted stir in cream and brandy with a whisk, making a smooth, thick mixture.
2. With a fondue fork, pierce a piece of sponge cake, lady finger, pineapple chunk, banana or apple. Dip in chocolate to cover. Transfer to another fork and eat.
3. You may use any other combination of sweets or fruits that you prefer, rather than those listed above.

CAFÉ BRÛLOT DIABOLIQUE

6 pieces of lump sugar
8 whole cloves
1 one-inch stick cinnamon
1 cut-up lemon peel
4 jiggers brandy, heated
1 quart hot demitasse coffee

1. Place sugar, cloves, cinnamon and lemon peel in a chafing dish with heat on. Pour cognac over sugar cubes. Ignite with a match and stir ingredients slowly until well blended.
2. After a minute or two, slowly pour in the hot black coffee and continue to stir.
3. To serve, strain into demitasse cups.
4. Makes 1 quart.

Fondue Bourguignonne

Quick Minestrone

Soups

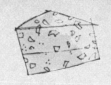

Soup is just plain wonderful! It is the first course of a formal dinner, a pick-me-up on a cold day, a lunch in itself, and even a complete dinner if it's a hearty meat-and-vegetable soup. Made in large quantities, it is good the first day, better the second, and can be frozen to use again weeks later.

MINESTRONE A LA MILANESE

¼ pound bacon
½ cup diced onion
1 clove garlic, quartered
6 beef bouillon cubes
6 cups boiling water
½ cup peeled, sliced carrots
½ cup diced celery
1 cup fresh green beans, cut in ½-inch slices
½ cup peeled, diced potatoes
1 cup sliced zucchini squash
1 cup shredded cabbage
3 medium tomatoes, peeled and diced
¼ cup chopped parsley
1 tablespoon salt
1 teaspoon basil leaves
½ teaspoon freshly ground pepper
 Grated Parmesan cheese

1. Place Dutch oven over medium heat. Add bacon and cook until bacon is browned and crisp. Remove bacon and drain on paper towels.
2. Add onion and garlic to bacon fat in Dutch oven and cook, stirring occasionally, until lightly browned.
3. Add bouillon cubes, water, carrots, celery, green beans, and potatoes. Reduce heat to low.
4. Cover with vac-control valve closed. Simmer 45 minutes.
5. Add squash, cabbage, tomatoes, parsley, salt, basil leaves and pepper. Cover and simmer 20 minutes. Crumble bacon and stir into hot soup.
6. Serve with Parmesan cheese sprinkled over the top.
7. Makes about 2 quarts.

QUICK MINESTRONE

6 beef bouillon cubes
6 cups hot water
1 cup red table wine
¼ pound bacon, cut in pieces
1½ cups cooked navy beans
2 cups shredded raw cabbage
1 cup diced raw potato
1 cup diced raw carrots
1 cup diced raw celery
1 cup minced onion
1 clove garlic, finely minced
1 can (1 pound) tomatoes
½ teaspoon seasoned salt
 Salt and pepper to taste
¼ pound elbow macaroni
 Grated Parmesan cheese

1. Dissolve bouillon cubes in hot water in Dutch oven. Add red wine, bacon, beans, cabbage, potato, carrots, celery, onion, garlic, tomatoes, seasoned salt, and salt and pepper to taste.
2. Place over medium heat and bring to a boil.
3. Reduce heat to low. Cover with vac-control valve closed. Simmer about 1 hour.
4. Add macaroni and simmer 20 minutes or until macaroni is tender.
5. Serve with lots of Parmesan cheese and toasted Italian bread.
6. Makes 8 to 10 servings.

HEARTY VEGETABLE SOUP

1½ pound beef soup meat
1 beef marrow bone
2 quarts water
4 teaspoons salt
2 teaspoons seasoned salt
¼ teaspoon pepper
4 celery stalks with leaves, sliced
8 carrots, peeled and cut in ½-inch slices
6 potatoes, peeled and diced
2 medium onions, thinly sliced
2 cans (1 pound each) tomatoes

1. Place soup meat and bone in Dutch oven. Add water, salt, seasoned salt, pepper and celery. Bring to a boil over medium heat.
2. Reduce heat to low. Cover with vac-control valve closed. Simmer about 1½ hours. During first ½ hour of simmering, remove cover and skim scum from top of liquid with a metal spoon. Discard scum.
3. Add carrots, potatoes and onions. Simmer 30 minutes.
4. Remove meat and bone from soup. Cut meat into cubes and return to soup. Remove marrow from bone and return to soup.
5. Add tomatoes to soup and continue to simmer 15 to 20 minutes.
6. Taste and adjust seasoning to taste before serving.
7. Makes about 12 servings.

Note: Any left-over soup may be poured into freezer containers, leaving "head room" for expansion. Freeze soup as quickly as possible. To serve, run hot water over container to loosen block of soup. Place in a saucepan and heat over very low heat. Stir soup occasionally.

SPEEDY GAZPACHO

1 can (10¾ ounces) condensed tomato soup
1 cup water
1 tablespoon olive oil
2 tablespoons wine vinegar
1 large clove garlic, finely minced
1 cup finely chopped cucumber
½ cup finely chopped green pepper
¼ cup finely chopped onion
Croutons

1. Combine soup, water, olive oil, vinegar and garlic in a bowl. Chill for 4 hours.
2. Serve in chilled bowls. Pass chilled cucumber, green pepper and onions. Top with crisp croutons.
3. Makes 2 to 3 servings.

HAMBURGER SOUP

2 tablespoons fat
1 pound ground chuck
1 cup canned tomatoes
½ cup peeled, diced carrots
½ cup diced celery
1 onion, chopped
2 teaspoons salt
¼ cup barley
½ teaspoon pepper
1½ cups water
1 potato, peeled and diced

1. Heat fat in 4-quart saucepan over medium heat. Add ground chuck and cook, stirring occasionally, until meat is browned.
2. Add remaining ingredients. Reduce heat to low.
3. Cover with vac-control valve closed. Simmer about 1½ hours.
4. Serve, garnished with chopped parsley if desired.
5. Makes about 6 servings.

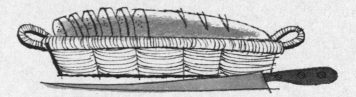

CHEESE AND ONION SOUP

¼ cup butter or margarine
1½ cups thinly sliced onions
2 tablespoons flour
4 cups milk
1 teaspoon salt
Dash of pepper
1 cup grated American cheese
Snipped parsley

1. Place butter in top part of double boiler. Add onions and cook over low heat, stirring occasionally, until onions are tender but not browned.
2. Remove from heat and stir in flour. Slowly stir in milk, until mixture is smooth. Cook over low heat, stirring constantly, until mixture is thickened and comes to a boil.
3. Put boiling water in bottom part of double boiler. Put top of double boiler in place. Add salt, pepper and cheese. Cook, stirring occasionally, until cheese melts and mixture is smooth.
4. Serve in bowls topped with snipped parsley.
5. Makes 4 servings.

90

SPLIT PEA SOUP

1 pound green split peas
1 ham bone
2½ quarts water
3 onions, chopped
2 carrots, peeled and diced
1 bay leaf
2 celery-stalk tops, chopped
3 sprigs parsley, chopped
Salt and pepper
¼ cup sherry

1. Wash peas and soak overnight if directions on package say to do so. Drain.
2. Place peas, ham bone, water, onion, carrots, bay leaf, celery tops, parsley, salt, and pepper in Dutch oven. Bring to a boil over medium-high heat.
3. Turn heat to low. Cover with vac-control valve closed. Simmer about 2 hours or until peas are mushy.
4. Remove ham bone. Remove any bits of ham from bone and reserve. Put soup through food press.
5. Return soup to Dutch oven. Add bits of ham. Heat thoroughly.
6. Just before serving stir in sherry and taste for seasoning, adding additional salt and pepper if needed.
7. Makes 3 quarts soup.

Note: Any left-over soup may be poured into freezer containers, leaving "head room" for expansion. Freeze soup as quickly as possible. To serve, run container under hot water to loosen soup. Place in a saucepan and heat over very low heat. Stir soup often to keep from sticking and scorching.

QUEBEC GREEN PEA SOUP

1 can (2 ounces) mushroom stems and pieces
1 tablespoon butter or margarine
2 cans (11¼ ounces each) condensed green pea soup
2 soup cans water and mushroom liquid
1 cup grated raw carrot

1. Drain mushrooms saving liquid to combine with water to make 2 cups liquid.
2. Melt butter in a saucepan. Add mushrooms and sauté a few minutes.
3. Add soup, water and mushroom liquid. Stir until smooth.
4. Add grated carrot. Bring to a boil; lower heat and simmer 10 minutes or until carrot is tender.
5. Makes 4 to 6 servings.

CREME DE POURRI

1 can (10½ ounces) condensed cream of mushroom soup
½ soup can water
½ soup can milk
¼ cup cooked peas
¼ cup diced, cooked left-over chicken
1 teaspoon Worcestershire sauce

1. Turn soup into a saucepan. Gradually blend in water and milk, stirring until mixture is smooth.
2. Add peas, chicken, and Worcestershire sauce.
3. Heat, over low heat, stirring occasionally. Do not boil soup.
4. Makes 2 to 3 servings.

LIMA BEAN SOUP

2 packages (1 pound each) dried lima beans
1 large onion, chopped
1 apple, peeled, cored and chopped
1 ham bone
2 teaspoons salt
¼ teaspoon pepper
½ teaspoon savory
4 frankfurters, sliced in rings

1. Soak lima beans several hours or overnight according to directions on package.
2. Drain beans and place in Dutch oven. Add onion, apple, ham bone, salt, pepper and savory. Add enough water to bring level of water 1 inch over top of beans.
3. Place over medium heat and bring to a boil. Reduce heat to low. Cover with vac-control valve closed. Simmer 1½ to 2 hours, stirring occasionally, or until beans are mushy.
4. Remove ham bone. Put soup mixture through food press. Return to Dutch oven. Remove any bits of ham from bone and add to soup mixture. Add frankfurter rings and heat thoroughly.
5. Makes 8 to 10 servings.

Note: Any left-over soup may be poured into freezer containers, leaving "head room" for expansion. Freeze soup as quickly as possible. To serve, run hot water over container to loosen block of soup. Place in a saucepan and heat over very low heat. Stir soup frequently to keep from sticking and scorching.

TURKEY SOUP

1 turkey carcass (turkey bones with all meat removed)
2 quarts cold water
2 teaspoons salt
¾ teaspoon Tabasco
2 sprigs parsley
2 celery stalks with leaves, cut up
2 onions, sliced
½ teaspoon basil
1 bay leaf
½ cup converted rice
1 cup thinly sliced carrot rings
1 cup diced cooked left over turkey

1. Break up the turkey carcass and place in Dutch oven or large soup kettle. Add any left-over gravy and giblets. Add water, salt, Tabasco, parsley, celery stalks, onions, basil, and bay leaf.
2. Bring to a boil over medium heat. Reduce heat to low.
3. Cover with vac-control valve closed. Simmer about 3 hours.
4. Remove from heat and let stand about 10 minutes. Strain turkey liquid through strainer into large saucepan. Let liquid stand about 15 minutes and skim off excess fat.
5. Bring liquid or turkey stock to a boil over medium heat. Add rice and carrot rings. Reduce heat to low.
6. Cover with vac-control valve closed. Simmer 15 minutes or until rice is tender. Add turkey pieces and heat thoroughly before serving.
7. Makes about 1½ quarts.

Note: Any left-over soup may be poured into freezer containers, leaving "head room" for expansion. Freeze soup as quickly as possible. To serve, run hot water over container to loosen block of soup. Place in a saucepan and heat over a very low heat. Stir soup occasionally.

COLD CUCUMBER SOUP

1 can (10½ ounces) condensed tomato soup
½ cucumber, peeled and sliced
¼ cup chopped green onions
½ teaspoon salt
Dash of pepper
½ cup medium cream
½ cup water

1. Place all ingredients in container of electric blender. Run until mixture is smooth.
2. Chill for several hours before serving.
3. Makes 4 servings.

VEGETABLE BEAN-POT SOUP

1 can (10½ ounces) condensed bean with bacon soup
1 can (10¾ ounces) condensed minestrone soup
2 soup cans water
½ cup diced salami
1 hard-cooked egg, sliced
Chopped parsley

1. In a saucepan combine soups and water. Add salami.
2. Place over medium heat and heat, stirring occasionally.
3. Ladle hot soup into soup bowls and garnish with hard-cooked egg slices and sprinkle with parsley.
4. Makes 4 to 6 servings.

COLD CURRIED CREAM OF VEGETABLE SOUP

1 can (10½ ounces) condensed cream of vegetable soup
1 package (3 ounces) cream cheese
½ teaspoon curry powder
1 soup can ice water

1. Keep can of soup in refrigerator 3 to 4 hours.
2. Soften cream cheese; blend in curry powder. Gradually add cold soup. Mix with ice water to desired consistency, one can or slightly less. Blend thoroughly.
3. Serve in chilled bowls.
4. Makes 2 to 3 servings.

COLD CURRIED CHICKEN SOUP

1 can (10½ ounces) condensed cream of chicken soup
¼ teaspoon curry powder
2 tablespoons snipped water cress leaves
Cold milk
Cherry tomatoes, sliced

1. Keep soup in refrigerator 3 to 4 hours.
2. Just before serving, open soup and turn into a chilled bowl. Stir in curry powder and water cress. Mix with cold milk to desired consistency, one can of milk or a little less.
3. Serve in chilled bowls. Garnish each serving with cherry tomato slices.
4. Makes 2 to 3 servings.

NEW ENGLAND CLAM CHOWDER

½ pound lean salt pork, finely diced
2 onions, chopped
3 medium potatoes, peeled and diced
2 cups hot water
2 cans (7½ ounces) minced clams
1 can (14½ ounces) evaporated milk
⅔ cup milk
Salt and pepper

1. Place 4-quart saucepan over medium heat. Add salt pork and cook, stirring occasionally until crisp.
2. Reduce heat to low. Add onions and cook, stirring occasionally, until onions are limp but not browned.
3. Add potatoes and hot water.
4. Cover with vac-control valve closed. Simmer about 15 minutes or until potatoes are tender.
5. Add clams and liquor from clams, evaporated milk and plain milk. Cook over low heat until hot but do not boil.
6. Season to taste with salt and pepper. Serve with crackers.
7. Makes 4 to 6 servings.

Note: This is very good if made early in the day, or even the day before, then refrigerated. Heat, but do not boil, just before serving.

LAMB AND BARLEY SOUP

2 to 3 lamb shanks
3 quarts water
½ teaspoon pepper corns
1 cup green split peas
½ cup uncooked barley
3 cups chopped carrots
1½ cups chopped onions
1½ cups chopped celery
¼ cup chopped parsley
Salt and pepper

1. Have butcher crack bones of lamb shanks. Wash shanks and cut off excess fat.
2. Place shanks in Dutch oven with water, peppercorns, peas and barley. Cover and simmer about 2 hours.
3. Add carrots, onions, celery and parsley. Simmer about 1 hour longer.
4. Let soup cool. Remove shanks and cut meat into small pieces. Skim fat from top of soup. Return meat to soup.
5. Reheat and season to taste with salt and pepper.
6. Makes 3 quarts soup.

CORN CHOWDER

½ cup diced salt pork or bacon
3 medium potatoes, peeled and finely diced
¼ cup minced onion
2 cups water
1 can (1 pound 4 ounces) cream-style corn
2 teaspoons salt
Pepper to taste
2 cups light cream, scalded

1. Cook pork in a saucepan over medium heat until brown and crisp. Add remaining ingredients except cream. Cover tightly and simmer 15 to 20 minutes or until potatoes are tender.
2. Stir in cream. Heat but do not boil.
3. Makes about 4 servings.

DOWN-EAST FISH CHOWDER

1 pound fish fillets, fresh or frozen
2 cups milk
1 cup light cream
1 cup crushed saltine crackers
4 slices bacon, cut in squares
1 medium onion, chopped
¼ cup sliced celery
1 cup water
1 cup peeled, diced potatoes
½ cup peeled, sliced carrots
1 bay leaf, crumbled
¼ cup butter or margarine
Salt and pepper to taste

1. If fish fillets are frozen allow them to thaw. Cut fish into bite-sized pieces.
2. Mix together milk, cream, and saltines in a bowl and set aside.
3. Place 4-quart saucepan over medium heat. Add bacon to saucepan and cook until lightly browned. Add onions and celery and cook until celery is limp but not browned.
4. Add water, potatoes, carrots and bay leaf. Reduce heat to low.
5. Cover with vac-control valve closed. Simmer 10 minutes, or until potatoes are tender.
6. Add fish pieces, milk-cracker mixture and butter. Cover and simmer 5 to 8 minutes or until fish flakes easily when tested with a fork. Season to taste with salt and pepper. Serve immediately.
7. Makes 6 to 8 servings.

Seafood

Seafood restaurants are popular eating-out places, yet too few people eat seafood in their own homes. Do the chefs have a secret? Yes, indeed, and it is perfectly simple: Don't overcook! Cook it too long, and it becomes dry, tasteless, unappetizing. Cook it properly, according to our recipes, and you will find that you've become the most popular seafood chef in town.

BOILED LOBSTER

1. Bring 3 quarts of water and 3 tablespoons of salt to a full rolling boil, in 6 qt. Dutch oven.
2. Drop into water a 1 to 1½ pound live lobster.
3. Cover with vac-control valve closed and return to boil. Cook 5 minutes for the first pound and 3 minutes for each additional pound.
4. Remove from boiling water immediately.
5. Rinse with cold water until lobster is cool enough to handle. Do not chill too much.
6. Place lobster on its back on a large cutting board.
7. Cross the large claws and hold firmly with the left hand. Insert the point of a sharp knife into the lobster at the head and cut the shell open from head to tail. Cut through to the back shell.
8. Remove the stomach and the intestinal vein that runs the length of the tail section close to the back. Do not remove juices, coral, or the liver. (The liver is the grayish looking meat found in the body cavity which turns green when it is cooked.)
9. Serve with melted butter blended with a squeeze of lemon juice. Supply nut crackers to crack claws.
10. Plan on 1 lobster per person.
11. One lobster makes one serving.

BAKED LOBSTER

  4 1½- to 2-pound lobsters
1½ cups cracker crumbs
  ½ teaspoon salt
  2 tablespoons Worcestershire sauce
  ½ cup melted butter or margarine, divided

1. Have fish dealer split and clean each lobster.
2. Heat oven to 450°F.
3. Combine cracker crumbs, salt, Worcestershire sauce and 4 tablespoons melted butter or margarine.
4. Place lobsters on baking sheets or baking pans. Fill body cavity with cracker crumb mixture. Pour additional melted butter or margarine over stuffing.
5. Bake 19 minutes.
6. Serve immediately with hot melted butter.
7. Makes 4 servings.

LOBSTER CANTONESE

  6 frozen rock lobster tails, thawed (6 to 8 ounces each)
  ¼ cup salad oil
  1 clove garlic, minced
  ½ pound ground pork
  2 tablespoons cornstarch
  ¼ cup soy sauce
  1 teaspoon sugar
  1 teaspoon salt
    Dash of pepper
2¼ cups chicken bouillon
  2 eggs
  ½ cup slivered green onions
    Hot cooked rice

1. Cut lobster tails crosswise in 1-inch sections.
2. Put salad oil in large skillet and heat over medium heat. Add garlic and pork. Cook, stirring occasionally, until pork is no longer pink, about 10 minutes.
3. While pork is cooking, combine cornstarch with ⅓ cup water in a small bowl. Add soy sauce, sugar, salt and pepper. Stir mixture into skillet with pork. Add bouillon and stir thoroughly. Bring mixture to a boil; reduce heat and simmer, stirring until thickened and clear.
4. Add lobster pieces, cover with vac-control valve closed and cook over low heat until lobster is tender, about 8 to 10 minutes.
5. Beat eggs slightly with a fork. Blend some of the hot lobster mixture into bowl with egg. Beat well. Stir egg mixture, all at once, into hot lobster mixture in skillet. Stir quickly, as eggs cook and form shreds in the mixture.
6. Add onions and serve immediately with hot cooked rice and additional soy sauce.
7. Makes 6 servings.

BOILED SHRIMP

1 pound raw shrimp
1 quart water
½ stalk celery
1 carrot, sliced
1 small onion, sliced
Juice of ½ lemon
1 teaspoon salt
½ teaspoon pepper

1. Shrimp may be shelled either before or after boiling. To clean shrimp, hold tail end in left hand, slip thumb under shell between legs and lift off 2 or 3 segments in one motion. Then still holding firmly to tail, pull out shrimp from remaining shell section and tail. With a knife, cut along outside curve and lift out black sand vein, if desired. Vein is harmless but some people object to the appearance of the black line.
2. Put water in a large saucepan. Add celery, carrot, onion, lemon juice, salt and pepper. Bring to a boil.
3. Add shrimp, let water come to a boil again. Turn heat down so that water just simmers. Cover saucepan with vac-control valve closed and let shrimp cook 5 minutes. Drain shrimp and cool quickly.

✳ ✳ ✳ ✳ ✳ ✳ ✳ ✳ ✳ ✳ ✳ ✳ ✳ ✳

SWEET AND PUNGENT SHRIMP

¼ cup brown sugar
2 tablespoons cornstarch
½ teaspoon salt
¼ cup vinegar
1 tablespoon soy sauce
1 can (No. 2) pineapple chunks
1 green pepper, cut in strips
1 onion, thinly sliced
1 pound shrimp, cooked and cleaned
Hot cooked rice

1. Combine sugar, cornstarch, salt, vinegar, soy sauce and the drained juice from pineapple in a saucepan.
2. Cook over low heat, stirring constantly, until slightly thickened. Add green pepper, onion, and pineapple chunks. Simmer about 5 minutes.
3. Remove from heat. Add shrimp. Cover with vac-control valve closed and let stand 10 minutes.
4. Just before serving, bring mixture to a boil, stirring constantly.
5. Serve with hot cooked rice.
6. Makes 4 servings.

ITALIAN SHRIMP

1½ pounds raw shrimp
5 tablespoons olive oil
¾ cup chopped onions
1 large clove garlic, crushed
2 tablespoons minced parsley
Pinch of thyme
½ teaspoon salt
Dash of freshly ground black pepper
1 can (2 pounds 3 ounces) Italian plum tomatoes
½ cup dry white wine
¾ tablespoon sugar
Hot cooked rice

1. Remove shells and black sand vein from shrimp.
2. Heat olive oil in a large skillet over medium-high heat.
3. Add onions, garlic, parsley and thyme. Cook until onions are limp but not browned.
4. Add shrimp, a few at a time. Cook lightly on both sides. Add salt and pepper. Add tomatoes, wine and sugar.
5. Cover with vac-control valve closed and simmer over low heat about 20 minutes or until sauce is slightly thickened.
6. Makes 6 servings.

SUPPER SHRIMP AND RICE

2 cups water
⅔ cup instant nonfat dry milk
¼ cup all-purpose flour
1½ teaspoon salt
⅛ teaspoon garlic salt
Freshly ground black pepper
3 tablespoons butter
¼ cup chopped celery
1 can (4 ounces) sliced button mushrooms
1 pound cooked and cleaned shrimp
Hot cooked rice

1. Pour water into top part of double boiler. Combine milk, flour, salt, garlic salt and a a dash of pepper. Sprinkle on surface of water and stir until blended. Cook over hot water, stirring occasionally, until mixture has thickened. Keep warm.
2. Melt butter in a small skillet over medium heat. Add celery and cook about 5 minutes or until celery is limp but not browned. Add mushrooms and cook about 2 minutes.
3. Turn mixture into sauce in double boiler. Add shrimp and heat thoroughly.
4. Serve piping hot with rice.
5. Makes 4 servings.

✳ ✳ ✳ ✳ ✳ ✳ ✳ ✳ ✳ ✳ ✳ ✳ ✳ ✳

SAUCY SCALLOPS

2 tablespoons butter or margarine
1 pound scallops, cut into bite-size pieces
¼ cup sliced green onions
1 can (10½ ounces) condensed cream of mushroom soup
¼ cup light cream
2 tablespoons dry white wine
1 tablespoon chopped parsley
¼ cup buttered bread crumbs
2 tablespoons grated Parmesan cheese

1. Heat butter in skillet over medium heat. Add scallops and onion and cook until onion is tender.
2. Stir in mushroom soup, cream, wine and parsley. Heat, stirring occasionally, but do not boil.
3. Spoon mixture into 4 individual baking dishes; sprinkle with crumbs and cheese. Place on rack in broiling compartment, about 3 inches from source of heat, and broil until crumbs are browned.
4. Makes 4 servings.

SEAFOOD NEWBURG

¼ cup butter
½ cup flour
6 cups milk
1½ teaspoons salt
½ teaspoon paprika
4 egg yolks
½ teaspoon Tabasco
4 cups cooked shellfish (shelled shrimp, lobster, or crabmeat, cut up)
Sherry, if desired

1. Melt butter in a saucepan. Add flour and stir to a smooth paste.
2. Remove from heat and stir in milk. Return to heat and cook, stirring constantly, until mixture comes to a boil and thickens. Add salt and pepper.
3. Beat egg yolks slightly in a small bowl. Stir a small amount of hot milk mixture into egg yolks, beating constantly. Return mixture to remaining sauce and stir thoroughly. Cook over low heat, stirring constantly, 3 minutes.
4. Remove from heat and stir in Tabasco. Beat mixture thoroughly with a rotary beater or a whisk.
5. Fold in seafood. Keep warm over hot water in top of a double boiler. Fold in 2 tablespoons sherry, if desired.
6. Serve on rice or toast points.
7. Makes 8 servings.

CHEESE AND LOBSTER

6 tablespoons butter or margarine
2 tablespoons flour
½ teaspoon paprika
2 cups light cream
1 package (6 ounces) American cheese slices, cut into thin strips
4 cups cooked lobster meat, cut into pieces
2 cans (4 ounces each) sliced mushrooms

1. Melt butter in blazer pan of chafing dish over direct flame. Blend in flour and paprika. Stir in cream and cheese.
2. Place blazer pan over hot water. Cook, stirring constantly, until cheese is melted and mixture thickens.
3. Add lobster and mushrooms. Cover. Cook until lobster and mushrooms are thoroughly heated, about 8 minutes.
4. Serve over toasted waffles or in patty shells.
5. Makes 8 servings.

PERCH ALMONDINE

1 package frozen ocean perch fillets
¼ cup flour
½ teaspoon salt
Dash of pepper
½ cup butter or margarine, divided
⅓ cup blanched slivered almonds
2 teaspoons lemon juice

1. Thaw fillets just enough to separate. Combine flour, salt and pepper. Roll fish in seasoned flour.
2. Melt ¼ cup of the butter in a skillet over medium heat. Add fillets and brown on both sides, about 8 to 10 minutes.
3. Meanwhile melt remaining butter in a saucepan. Add almonds and cook until delicately browned.
3. Arrange fried fillets on a heated platter. Top with cooked almonds and sprinkle with lemon juice.
4. Makes 4 servings.

SHRIMP MARINARA

1 pound shrimp, fresh or frozen
2 tablespoons salad oil
¼ cup chopped celery
¼ teaspoon garlic salt
1 teaspoon oregano
¼ teaspoon salt
⅛ teaspoon cayenne
¼ teaspoon sugar
½ teaspoon basil
2 tablespoons chopped parsley
1 can (No. 2½) tomatoes
   Hot cooked rice

1. Shell and clean shrimp. Do not cook.
2. Heat salad oil in a large skillet. Add celery and cook over low heat until tender.
3. Add remaining ingredients, except shrimp, and cook over low heat, stirring occasionally, until liquid is reduced and mixture is slightly thickened, about 30 minutes.
4. Add shrimp. Cover skillet with vac-control valve closed and let cook 5 to 8 minutes, depending on size of shrimp.
5. Serve with hot cooked rice.
6. Makes 4 servings.

FISH FILLET PUFFS

1 package frozen fish fillets
   Salt and pepper
1 egg white
¼ cup mayonnaise
1 teaspoon minced onion
¼ teaspoon Worcestershire sauce
   Dash of Tabasco

1. Heat oven to 425°F.
2. Let fillets thaw on shelf of refrigerator or at room temperature.
3. Separate fillets and arrange skin side down in a shallow buttered baking dish. Season with salt and pepper.
4. Beat egg white until stiff but not dry. Fold in mayonnaise, onion, Worcestershire and Tabasco. Spread sauce on fish fillets.
5. Bake 18 to 20 minutes or until fish flakes easily when tested with a fork and sauce is golden brown.
6. Makes 4 servings.

LOBSTER ARTICHOKE BAKE

½ cup thinly sliced celery
1 large clove garlic, minced
2 tablespoons butter or margarine
2 cans (10½ ounces each) condensed cream of mushroom soup
¼ cup light cream
2 cups cut-up cooked lobster
1 package (9 ounces) frozen artichoke hearts, cooked, drained and cut in half
3 tablespoons sherry
2 tablespoons chopped pimiento
½ teaspoon paprika
⅓ cup bread crumbs
3 tablespoons melted butter
2 tablespoons grated Parmesan cheese

1. Cook celery and garlic in butter in a large saucepan, over medium heat, until tender but not browned.
2. Add soup, cream, lobster, artichokes, sherry, pimiento and paprika. Heat over low heat, stirring often, until mixture is piping hot.
3. Pour into 6 individual shallow baking dishes.
4. Combine crumbs, butter and cheese. Sprinkle over lobster mixture.
5. Place on rack in broiler about 5 inches from source of heat. Broil until topping is browned.
6. Makes 4 to 6 servings.

LOBSTER-SHRIMP THERMIDOR

1 tablespoon butter or margarine
1 can (4 ounces) sliced mushrooms, drained
1 cup diced cooked lobster or 1 can (6 ounces) lobster, drained
1 can (10 ounces) frozen condensed cream of shrimp soup
¼ cup milk
¼ teaspoon dry mustard
   Dash cayenne pepper
   Grated Parmesan cheese
   Paprika

1. Melt butter in a saucepan over medium heat. Add drained mushrooms and brown lightly. Add diced lobster and cook a few minutes.
2. Stir in soup, milk, mustard and cayenne. Heat slowly, stirring occasionally, until soup is thawed and mixture is hot.
3. Heat oven to 400°F.
4. Spoon lobster mixture into 3 individual baking dishes. Sprinkle cheese and paprika on top.
5. Bake 15 minutes or until hot and bubbly.
6. Makes 3 servings.

PAN-SAUTEED SCALLOPS

1½ pounds scallops
1 cup dry bread crumbs
¼ cup butter or margarine
¼ teaspoon salt
⅛ teaspoon pepper
  Pinch of paprika
3 tablespoons dry white wine
  Toast

1. If scallops are large, cut in halves or quarters. Roll in dry bread crumbs.
2. Melt butter in skillet. Heat over medium-high heat but do not allow to smoke. Add scallops, salt, pepper and paprika and cook 5 minutes, turning constantly.
3. Remove scallops from pan and keep hot. Lower heat and add wine to drippings in skillet. Stir and heat.
4. Arrange scallops on toast and pour hot sauce over top.
5. Makes 4 to 6 servings.

CREAMED SCALLOPS

1½ pounds fresh sea scallops, cut into bite-size cubes
⅓ cup water
3 tablespoons butter or margarine
1½ tablespoons cornstarch
¾ teaspoon salt
¼ teaspoon pepper
1 tablespoon finely chopped green pepper
1 teaspoon finely chopped onion
1½ cups milk
1 tablespoon chopped parsley
1 tablespoon lemon juice

1. Combine scallops and water in a saucepan. Cover with vac-control valve closed and bring to a boil. Reduce heat to low and simmer 2 to 5 minutes or until tender. Drain.
2. Melt butter in a saucepan. Blend in cornstarch, salt and pepper. Add green pepper and onion. Remove from heat.
3. Gradually add milk, stirring until smooth. Return to heat and cook over medium heat, stirring constantly, until mixture thickens and comes to a boil.
4. Add parsley, lemon juice and scallops. Heat thoroughly.
5. Serve over toast.
6. Makes 6 servings.

TOMATO FISH FILLETS

6 fish fillets
¼ cup tartar sauce
7 sticks American cheese
1 can (8 ounces) tomato sauce
⅔ cup dry bread crumbs
  Salt and pepper
2 tablespoons butter or margarine

1. Heat oven to 375°F.
2. Spread fish fillets with tartar sauce. Roll each fillet around a stick of cheese and fasten with toothpicks. Place in a baking dish.
3. Pour tomato sauce over fish. Sprinkle with bread crumbs and season with salt and pepper. Dot with botter.
4. Bake 25 to 30 minutes or until fish flakes easily when tested with a fork.
5. Makes 6 servings.

FISH STEAKS IN WINE SAUCE

4 fish steaks
1 can (10½ ounces) condensed tomato soup
⅓ cup red wine
1 jar (4 ounces) pimiento cheese spread
2 tablespoons chopped parsley
1 teaspoon minced onion

1. Heat oven to 375°F.
2. Arrange fish steaks in a shallow baking dish.
3. Combine soup, wine and cheese in a saucepan. Cook and stir over low heat until cheese melts. Stir in parsley and onion.
4. Pour over steaks in baking dish.
5. Bake about 25 minutes or until fish flakes easily when tested with a fork.
6. Makes 4 servings.

OVEN-FRIED FISH STEAKS

4 fish steaks
1 cup milk
2 teaspoons salt
  Dash of pepper
½ cup fine dry bread crumbs
¼ cup melted butter or margarine

1. Heat oven to 500°F.
2. If steaks are frozen, thaw on shelf of refrigerator or at room temperature.
3. Combine milk with salt and pepper. Spread bread crumbs on waxed paper. Dip steaks in milk then in crumbs. Place in a buttered shallow baking dish. Drizzle melted butter on top of steaks.
4. Bake 10 to 12 minutes or until fish flakes easily when tested with a fork.
5. Makes 4 servings.

Quick Breads

The aroma of home-baked bread is sure to bring back the happiest childhood memories—visits to grandmother's house, or rainy days helping mother bake fresh rolls for supper. Today, with easy short cuts and a wide variety of quick mixes available, it is no trick at all to prepare them for any meal.

MUFFINS

2 cups sifted flour
3 teaspoons double-acting baking powder
½ teaspoon salt
2 tablespoons sugar
1 egg
1 cup milk
¼ cup salad oil or melted shortening

1. Heat oven to 425°F.
2. Butter 14 2½-inch muffin pan cups.
3. Sift flour, baking powder, salt and sugar into a bowl.
4. Beat egg in another bowl; stir in milk and salad oil and mix well.
5. Make a well in center of flour mixture. Pour in milk mixture. Stir quickly until batter is just mixed, but still lumpy.
6. Fill muffin cups two-thirds full.
7. Bake 25 minutes or until a cake tester, inserted in center of muffin comes out clean.
8. Run a knife around each muffin to loosen. Place on heated dish or in a basket, covered with a cloth.
9. Makes 12 to 14 muffins.

VARIATIONS

Surprise Muffins: Fill greased muffin cups half full of batter; drop a scant teaspoon of jelly or jam on center of each; add more batter to fill cups two-thirds full.
Orange Muffins: Increase sugar to ¼ cup. Reduce milk to ¾ cup. With milk, add ¼ cup orange juice and 1 teaspoon grated orange rind.
Muffins Plus: Add ½ cup light or dark raisins. Add 1 cup finely chopped walnuts. Add 1 cup cut-up pitted dates.

BAKING POWDER BISCUITS

2 cups sifted flour
1 tablespoon double-acting baking powder
½ teaspoon salt
¼ cup shortening
⅔ to ¾ cup milk

1. Heat oven to 450°F.
2. Sift together flour, baking powder and salt into a large bowl. Cut in shortening with a pastry blender or two knives until the mixture is the consistency of corn meal. Add milk and stir only until a soft dough is formed. Start with ⅔ cup and add more milk if needed.
3. Turn mixture out onto a piece of waxed paper and press dough together with hands.
4. Place dough on a lightly floured board and knead 6 to 10 times. Roll dough out with a lightly floured rolling pin to ½-inch thickness. Dip a 2-inch biscuit cutter in flour and cut out rounds of dough. Place about 2 inches apart on a baking sheet. Shape pieces of left over dough into balls and flatten slightly. Place on baking sheet.
5. Bake 15 minutes or until lightly browned.

* * * * * * * * * * * * * * *

SOUR CREAM BISCUITS

2 cups sifted flour
1 tablespoon baking powder
¼ teaspoon baking soda
1 teaspoon salt
1 cup dairy sour cream
¼ cup milk

1. Heat oven to 450°F.
2. Sift flour, baking powder, baking soda and salt together into a bowl. Blend in sour cream. Stir in milk to make a soft dough.
3. Put a small amount of flour on a board or counter top. Turn dough out of bowl. Knead gently for a few minutes.
4. Roll or pat out dough to ½-inch thick. Cut out biscuits with a lightly floured biscuit cutter.
5. Place biscuits on a very lightly buttered baking sheet. Bake 10 minutes or until lightly browned on top.
6. Makes about 12 biscuits.

COFFEE CAKE

¾ cup butter or margarine
1¼ cups sugar, divided
2 eggs
1 teaspoon vanilla
2 cups sifted all-purpose flour
1 teaspoon baking powder
1 teaspoon baking soda
½ teaspoon salt
1 cup dairy sour cream
¼ cup brown sugar, firmly packed
½ teaspoon cinnamon

1. Heat oven to 350°F.
2. In a mixing bowl cream together butter and 1 cup of the sugar until light and fluffy. Beat in eggs, one at a time. Blend in vanilla.
3. Sift together flour, baking powder, baking soda and salt. Add to creamed mixture alternately with sour cream, beginning and ending with dry ingredients.
4. Spread batter evenly in a buttered 9-inch square pan.
5. In a small bowl combine remaining ¼ cup sugar, brown sugar and cinnamon. Sprinkle over top of batter.
6. Bake 45 to 55 minutes or until top springs back when lightly touched with the fingers.
7. Cool on a wire rack before serving.
8. Makes 9 servings.

SHERRIED COFFEE CAKE

2 cups biscuit mix
¼ cup sugar
2 tablespoons melted butter or margarine
¼ cup sherry
1 egg, beaten
½ cup milk
1 can (1 pound, 9½ ounces) apple pie filling
Sherry-Cinnamon Topping

1. Heat over to 400°F.
2. Combine biscuit mix and sugar in a mixing bowl. Combine butter, sherry, egg, and milk; beat lightly. Make a well in center of biscuit mix. Pour in milk mixture. Stir quickly just until batter is mixed, but still lumpy.
3. Turn mixture into a greased 9-inch square pan. Spread apple pie filling over top. Sprinkle Sherry-Cinnamon Topping over apples.
4. Bake about 35 minutes or until topping springs back when lightly touched with the fingers.
5. Serve warm.
6. Makes 8 to 9 servings.

SHERRY-CINNAMON TOPPING

½ cup biscuit mix
¼ cup brown sugar, firmly packed
½ teaspoon cinnamon
2 tablespoons melted butter or margarine
⅓ cup sherry

1. Combine biscuit mix, brown sugar and cinnamon. Stir in butter and sherry until well blended.
2. Use to sprinkle over top of coffee cake.

BATTER ROLLS

¾ cup milk
¼ cup sugar
1 teaspoon salt
¼ cup butter or margarine
½ cup warm water (105-115°F)
2 packages or cakes yeast, active dry or compressed
1 egg
3½ cups unsifted flour

1. Place milk in a saucepan over medium heat and heat just until bubbles appear around the edge of the pan. Remove from heat and stir in sugar, salt and butter.
2. Measure warm water into a large warm bowl. Sprinkle or crumble in yeast. Stir until dissolved. Add lukewarm milk mixture, egg and 2 cups of the flour. Beat until smooth. Stir in enough remaining flour to make a soft dough.
3. Cover bowl and let stand in a warm place, free from draft, until doubled in bulk, about 30 minutes.
4. Punch dough down with the hands. Shape into 24 rolls. Place on a greased baking sheet, in cake pans or in muffin cups. Cover and let rise in a warm place, free from draft, until doubled in bulk, about 30 minutes.
5. Heat oven to 400°F.
6. Bake rolls about 15 minutes or until lightly browned.
7. Makes 2 dozen rolls.

EASY DANISH KRINGLE

1 package (9½ ounces) refrigerator flaky
  biscuits
⅓ cup butter or margarine, melted
½ cup light brown sugar, firmly packed
1 cup finely chopped pecans
  Confectioners' sugar

1. Heat oven to 375°F.
2. Open biscuits according to package directions.
3. Place biscuits on a well-floured board in two rows with sides touching. With fingers, press or pinch the dough together, joining all edges. Use a drop of water to seal the biscuits.
4. With a well-floured rolling pin, roll dough out to a 20- by 10-inch rectangle; press to even sides.
5. Blend together ¼ cup of the melted butter, sugar and nuts. Spread mixture lengthwise over center of dough to a 3½-inch width. Fold one side of dough over filling; moisten lightly with water; overlap the other side of dough. Pinch edges of dough securely together. Fold each end up and seal well.
7. Place sealed-edge down on an ungreased baking sheet. Carefully shape into a horseshoe. Brush with remaining melted butter.
8. Bake 20 to 25 minutes, or until golden brown. Place on a cake rack to cool. Sprinkle lightly with confectioners' sugar.
9. Makes one 10-inch kringle.

QUICK CARAMEL BUNS

½ cup light brown sugar, firmly packed
⅓ cup butter, melted
1 tablespoon light corn syrup
½ cup coarsely chopped walnuts
1 package (9½ ounces) refrigerator flaky
  biscuits

1. Heat oven to 375°F.
2. In a small mixing bowl blend together sugar, butter, syrup and walnuts. Spoon a heaping tablespoon of the mixture into each of ten 3-inch muffin pan cups.
3. Open biscuits according to package directions. Place one biscuit in each cup on top of mixture.
4. Bake 12 to 14 minutes or until tops are golden brown.
5. Remove from oven and immediately invert muffin pan onto a large piece of foil; let pan remain over buns for 1 minute. Gently remove pan. Let buns cool.
6. Makes 10 buns.

PIZZA DOUGH

2½ to 3 cups unsifted flour
1½ teaspoons sugar
2 teaspoons salt
1 package active dry yeast
1 cup very hot tap water
2 tablespoons salad oil

1. In a large bowl thoroughly combine 1 cup of the flour, sugar, salt and active dry yeast. Gradually add very hot tap water and salad oil to dry ingredients and beat 1 minute at low speed with electric mixer, scraping bowl occasionally.
2. Stir in enough additional flour to make a soft dough.
3. Turn out onto a lightly floured board; knead until smooth and elastic, about 8 to 10 minutes.
4. Place dough in a greased bowl, turning to grease top. Cover and let rise in a warm place, free from draft, until doubled in bulk, about 45 minutes.
5. Punch dough down and divide in half. Press each piece of dough into a greased 12-inch pizza pan, forming a standing rim of dough. These may also be shaped on a greased baking sheet, forming a standing rim of dough.
6. Fill with desired filling and bake as directed.
7. Makes enough dough for 2 pizzas.

SHRIMP AND PEPPER PIZZA

1 cup chopped green pepper
⅓ cup chopped onion
¼ cup salad oil
1 can (8 ounces) tomato sauce
¼ cup water
1½ teaspoons salt
1 teaspoon oregano
1 teaspoon Worcestershire sauce
1 package (7 ounces) frozen shrimp, cooked
1 unbaked pizza crust
1 tablespoon grated Parmesan cheese

1. Heat oven to 350°F.
2. Cook green pepper and chopped onion in hot salad oil until tender. Stir in tomato sauce, water, salt, oregano and Worcestershire sauce. Bring mixture to a boil. Lower heat and simmer about 5 minutes.
3. Stir in shrimp. Spread on pizza crust. Sprinkle with cheese.
4. Bake 30 to 35 minutes or until done.
5. Makes 1 pizza.

CHEESE PIZZA

1 can (8 ounces) tomato sauce
1 tablespoon minced onion
½ teaspoon oregano
½ teaspoon salt
¼ teaspoon pepper
2 unbaked pizza crusts
½ cup grated Parmesan cheese
½ pound thinly sliced Mozzarella cheese

1. Heat oven to 425°F.
2. Combine tomato sauce, minced onion, oregano, salt and pepper. Spread half of the mixture over the top of each pizza crust.
3. Sprinkle with Parmesan cheese. Arrange slices of Mozzarella cheese over the top.
4. Bake 20 to 25 minutes or until browned and bubbly.
5. Makes 2 pizzas.

VARIATIONS

Hamburger Pizza: Brown ¼ pound ground chuck in a skillet over medium high heat. Combine with tomato sauce and seasonings. Proceed according to directions for Cheese Pizza.

Spicy Pizza: Before baking Cheese Pizza, top with small slices of hot sausage, cut-up slices of hot salami, or strips of anchovy.

WAGON WHEEL PIZZA

1 can (1 pound) pork and beans with tomato sauce
¼ cup catsup
1 teaspoon onion salt
1 unbaked pizza crust
4 slices American cheese, cut in half
4 frankfurters, cut lengthwise
2½ tablespoons pickle relish

1. Heat oven to 375°F.
2. In a saucepan combine beans, catsup, and onion salt. Bring to a boil, reduce heat and simmer about 3 minutes.
3. Remove from heat and cool slightly. Spread on pizza crust.
3. Arrange cheese on pie to resemble spokes of a wheel. Place a frankfurter half on top of each cheese slice, cut side down. Lightly score each frankfurter and sprinkle with relish.
4. Bake 30 to 35 minutes or until done.
5. Makes 1 pizza.

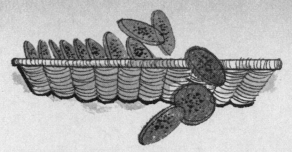

MUSHROOM HAMBURGER PIZZA PIE

3 tablespoons butter
½ pound mushrooms, sliced
½ cup minced onion
½ teaspoon Tabasco
1 can (8 ounces) tomato sauce
1 can (6 ounces) tomato paste
½ teaspoon oregano
½ teaspoon salt
1½ pounds ground beef
½ pound Mozzarella cheese, grated
2 unbaked pizza crusts

1. Heat oven to 450°F.
2. Melt butter in the skillet over medium-high heat. Add mushrooms and onion and cook until tender but not browned. Add Tabasco, tomato sauce, tomato paste, oregano and salt.
3. Cook beef in a skillet over medium-high heat. stirring with a fork until meat is broken up and has lost its red color. Add cooked beef to tomato mixture and simmer 5 minutes.
4. Arrange ¼ of the cheese on top of each pizza. Spread with ½ of the tomato meat mixture and top with remaining cheese.
5. Bake 15 to 20 minutes or until dough is golden brown and cheese is bubbly.
6. Makes 2 pizzas.

POPOVERS

2 eggs
1 cup milk
1 cup sifted all-purpose flour
¼ teaspoon salt

1. Heat oven to 425°F.
2. Thoroughly butter 6 large custard cups or iron popover pans. Place in oven and heat while preparing batter.
3. Beat eggs slightly. Beat in milk. Add flour and salt. Beat vigorously with an electric beater or rotary beater for 2 minutes.
4. Fill heated custard cups two-thirds full.
5. Bake about 40 minutes or until browned and well puffed. Do not open oven door during first 30 minutes of baking time.
6. Remove popovers and serve at once.
7. Makes 6 large popovers.

BANANA WALNUT BREAD

⅓ cup shortening
⅔ cup sugar
2 eggs, slightly beaten
⅓ cup chopped walnuts
1¾ cups sifted all-purpose flour
1¾ teaspoons baking powder
½ teaspoon salt
1 cup mashed ripe bananas

1. Heat oven to 350°F.
2. Grease the bottom of a 8½- by 4½- by 3-inch loaf pan.
3. Cream shortening until light and glossy. Gradually add sugar and beat until light and fluffy. Add eggs and beat until very well blended.
4. Fold in chopped walnuts.
5. Sift together flour, baking powder and salt. Add to egg mixture alternately with mashed bananas, blending thoroughly after each addition.
6. Turn batter into baking pan. Bake 60 to 70 minutes or until a cake tester inserted in the center of the loaf comes out clean.
7. Cool bread about 10 minutes in the pan and then turn out on rack to cool.
8. Makes one loaf.

DATE NUT LOAF BREAD

2 cups sifted flour
¼ cup sugar
1 tablespoon baking powder
½ teaspoon salt
1 egg, beaten
½ cup milk
½ cup light or dark corn syrup
2 tablespoons corn oil
½ cup chopped nuts
½ cup chopped dates

1. Heat oven to 350°F.
2. Grease a 9½- by 5½- by 3-inch loaf pan.
3. Sift together flour, sugar, baking powder and salt into a mixing bowl.
4. In another bowl combine egg, milk, corn syrup and corn oil.
5. Pour liquid ingredients into dry ingredients and mix just enough to blend. Do not over-mix.
6. Pour batter into prepared loaf pan. Bake 50 to 55 minutes or until a cake tester inserted in the center of the loaf comes out clean.
7. Cool bread about 10 minutes in the pan and and then turn out on rack to cool.
8. Makes one loaf.

PARSLEY-BUTTERED BREAD

¼ pound butter or margarine, melted
¼ teaspoon salt
⅛ teaspoon pepper
2 tablespoons chopped parsely
1 loaf French or Italian bread

1. Heat oven to 325°F.
2. Combine butter with seasonings. Cut bread into half-inch slices. Brush both sides of slices with butter mixture. Assemble slices in loaf form. Wrap loaf in foil.
3. Heat in oven about 20 minutes or until piping hot.

GARLIC BREAD

¼ pound butter or margarine, softened
3 cloves garlic, put through a garlic press
1 loaf French or Italian bread

1. Heat oven to 350°F.
2. Blend together butter and garlic. Cut bread into half-inch slices. Spread butter on one slice of bread, then top with another. Assemble loaf on a baking sheet by pressing slices together with butter mixture between each slice.
3. Heat about 15 minutes or until piping hot.

ORANGE HONEY CUBES

1 loaf unsliced day-old white bread
¼ cup light brown sugar
¾ teaspoon cinnamon
2 tablespoons frozen orange juice concentrate, undiluted
2 tablespoons honey
¼ cup melted butter or margarine
¼ cup coarsely chopped nuts

1. Heat oven to 350°F.
2. Cut crust from top and sides of bread. Cut bread lengthwise almost through to bottom crust, then cut crosswise to form 8 cubes.
3. Combine sugar, cinnamon, orange juice, honey, melted butter and nuts. Stir until well blended. Pour mixture over bread, letting some run down into cubes and over top. Tie loosely with a string.
4. Place on a baking sheet. Bake 10 to 15 minutes.
5. Remove string and serve warm.
6. Makes 6 servings.

Pineapple Skillet Cake

Desserts

Dinner would be incomplete without dessert. Cakes are easy to make with the new mixing methods and the wide selection of mixes on the market. Cookies are a breeze. As for pies, you can easily master the trick of flaky pastry, or purchase a frozen pastry shell all ready to be filled and baked. Fruits are part of the most luscious desserts, and with just a little practice you can bake a delicious upside-down cake in the skillet on top of your range.

PINEAPPLE SKILLET CAKE

½ cup butter or margarine, divided
1⅔ cups firmly packed brown sugar, divided
8 slices pineapple
8 maraschino cherries
2 cups sifted all-purpose flour
2 teaspoons baking powder
½ teaspoon salt
2 eggs
⅔ cup milk
1 teaspoon vanilla

1. Melt ¼ cup of the butter in the skillet over low heat. Cover butter with ⅔ cup of the brown sugar. Arrange pineapple slices on brown sugar. Place 1 cherry in the center of each pineapple slice.
2. Sift together flour, baking powder, and salt into a bowl.
3. Beat eggs in a small bowl. Beat in remaining cup of brown sugar until mixture is smooth and slightly stiff. Beat in milk and vanilla. Melt remaining ¼ cup butter and beat into eggs.
4. Pour egg mixture into bowl with dry ingredients. Beat until mixture is smooth, scraping down bowl with rubber scraper occasionally.
5. Carefully spoon batter over pineapple slices.
6. Cover with vac-control valve closed. Place over low heat and bake 40 minutes or until top springs back when lightly touched with fingers. Remove cover and let stand 2 minutes.
7. Cut around side of cake with a knife. Invert a large platter on top of skillet. Turn over and let stand 1 minute. Remove skillet. Scrape any syrup out of bottom of skillet and place on cake.
8. Serve warm or cold with whipped cream, if desired.

BANANA NUT CAKE

1⅔ cups sifted all-purpose flour
1 teaspoon baking soda
½ teaspoon salt
½ cup soft butter or margarine
1 cup granulated sugar
2 eggs
1 teaspoon vanilla extract
½ cup dairy sour cream
1 cup mashed bananas
1 cup finely chopped walnuts
Whipped cream

1. Place cover on skillet with vac-control valve closed. Let skillet stand over low heat while preparing cake batter.
2. Sift together flour, baking soda, and salt. Set aside.
3. In a large bowl put butter, sugar, eggs and vanilla extract. With electric mixer at high speed, beat 2 minutes or until mixture is light and fluffy. Add sour cream, bananas and walnuts. Beat well on low speed. Add flour mixture and beat at low speed until batter is well blended.
4. Brush bottom and sides of heated skillet with soft shortening. Sprinkle lightly with flour and brush onto bottom and sides, using a pastry brush.
5. Pour cake batter into skillet. Cover and bake 30 minutes. Open vac-control valve and bake 5 minutes longer or until top of cake is no longer moist.
6. Remove cover and turn off heat. Let cake cool in skillet.
7. Cut in pie shaped wedges and serve with sweetened whipped cream.
8. Makes 10 to 12 servings.

Lattice-Top Cherry Pie

Strawberry Glaze Pie

Peach Pie

GINGERBREAD PEACH UPSIDE-DOWN CAKE

¼ cup butter or margarine
1 cup brown sugar, firmly packed
1 can (1 pound, 4 ounces) peach slices
1 package (14.5 ounces) gingerbread mix

1. Melt butter in the skillet over low heat. Sprinkle brown sugar over top of butter. Drain peach slices and arrange on top of brown sugar.
2. Prepare gingerbread mix according to directions on package. Carefully spoon over peaches.
3. Cover with vac-control valve closed. Place over low heat and bake 30 minutes or until top springs back when lightly touched with fingers. Remove cover and let stand 2 minutes.
4. Cut around side of cake with a knife. Invert a large platter on top of skillet. Turn over and let stand 1 minute. Remove skillet. Scrape any syrup out of bottom of skillet and place on cake.
5. Serve warm or cold with whipped cream, if desired.

ELEGANT WALNUT DEVIL'S FOOD CAKE

1 cup walnuts
Butter or margarine
Granulated sugar
2 cups sifted cake flour
1 tablespoon instant coffee powder
1¾ cups granulated sugar
¾ cup cocoa
1¼ teaspoons baking soda
½ teaspoon baking powder
1 teaspoon salt
¾ cup shortening
1¼ cups milk, divided
2 teaspoons vanilla
3 eggs
Fluffy Cream Cheese Icing

1. Heat oven to 350°F.
2. Chop walnuts very fine. Generously butter sides and bottoms of two 9-inch layer cake pans. Sprinkle with granulated sugar. Sprinkle chopped walnuts evenly over bottom of each pan. Set aside.
3. Sift flour, coffee powder, sugar, cocoa, baking soda, baking powder, and salt into a large mixing bowl. Add shortening, ¾ cup milk, and vanilla. Beat two minutes with an electric mixer at medium speed, scraping bowl and beater often, or beat vigorously by hand about 150 strokes per minute.

4. Add eggs and remaining ½ cup milk. Beat 2 minutes longer.
5. Carefully spoon batter into walnut-coated pans. Bake 40 to 45 minutes or until a cake tester or toothpick inserted in the center of the cake comes out clean.
6. Let cakes stand a minute or two. Turn out onto wire racks to cool.
7. When cake is cold, spread some of the Fluffy Cream Cheese Icing between layers, putting the walnut coated sides together in center.
8. Frost sides and top of cake with remaining icing and sprinkle walnuts over the top, if desired.
9. Let cake stand until icing is set before cutting.
10. Makes one large cake of 10 to 12 servings.

FLUFFY CREAM CHEESE ICING

2 packages (3 ounces each) cream cheese
¼ cup soft butter
1 tablespoon instant coffee powder
⅛ teaspoon salt
¼ cup cream
4 cups sifted confectioners' sugar

1. Beat cheese until soft. Add butter, coffee powder, salt, cream, and confectioners' sugar. Beat well until smooth and creamy.
2. Spread on cooled Elegant Walnut Devil's Food Cake.

FANCY CAKE

1 package (1 pound, 3 ounces) yellow cake mix
¾ cup salad oil
¾ cup apricot nectar
1 package (3 ounces) lemon flavored gelatin
4 eggs
1 tablespoon lemon extract

1. Heat oven to 350°F.
2. In a large mixing bowl combine cake mix, salad oil, apricot nectar, and gelatin. Blend together.
3. Add eggs, one at a time, and beat thoroughly with an electric mixer after each egg. Beat in lemon extract.
4. Pour mixture into an ungreased angel food cake pan.
5. Bake 45 minutes or until a cake tester or toothpick inserted in cake comes out clean.
6. Invert angel food cake pan on rack and let cake cool thoroughly before removing from pan.
7. This cake is excellent plain or frosted.

1-2-3 PASTRY
One-Crust Pie

1⅓ cups sifted flour
½ teaspoon salt
⅓ cup salad oil
2 tablespoons cold water

1. Sift together flour and salt into a mixing bowl. Pour salad oil into flour and stir with a fork. Add cold water all at once and stir with a fork until dough is formed. Press dough firmly into a ball with hands. If mixture is too dry to form a ball, mix in 1 to 2 more tablespoons salad oil.
2. Flatten dough slightly with hands. Place dough between two squares of waxed paper. Roll dough into a 12-inch circle with a rolling pin. Wipe table with a damp cloth to keep waxed paper from slipping while rolling out dough.
3. Peel off top piece of paper. Place pastry in pie pan, paper side up. Gently peel off waxed paper. Fit pastry loosely into pan. Do not pull or stretch pastry.
4. Fold edges of crust under to make a stand-up rim of pastry. Flute edges of pastry by pressing the index finger of one hand between thumb and index finger of other hand.
5. For a baked shell, prick bottom and sides thoroughly with a fork. Bake in a very hot oven (450°F) 12 to 15 minutes or until light golden brown.
6. If the crust and filling are to be baked together, do not prick crust. Fill and bake as directed in the recipe.

1-2-3 PASTRY
Two-Crust Pie

2 cups sifted flour
1 teaspoon salt
½ cup salad oil
3 tablespoons cold water

1. Sift together flour and salt into a mixing bowl. Pour salad oil into flour and stir with a fork. Add cold water all at once and stir with a fork until dough is formed. Press dough firmly into a ball with hands. If mixture is too dry to form a ball, mix in 1 to 2 more tablespoons salad oil.
2. Divide dough roughly in half, using larger half for bottom pastry.
3. Flatten dough slightly with hands. Place dough between two squares of waxed paper. Roll dough into a 12-inch circle with a rolling pin. Wipe table with a damp cloth

to keep waxed paper from slipping while rolling out dough.
4. Peel off top piece of paper. Place pastry in pie pan, paper side up. Gently peel off waxed paper. Fit pastry loosely into pan. Do not pull or stretch pastry. Fill as desired.
5. Roll dough in similar manner for top crust. Place over filling. Trim 1 inch beyond rim of pan. Fold top layer of dough under bottom layer of dough and pinch together to seal. Flute edges of pastry by pressing the index finger of one hand between thumb and index finger of other hand. Cut slits in top.
6. Bake pies as directed in desired recipe.

STRAWBERRY GLAZE PIE

1 quart ripe strawberries
¾ cup water
1 cup sugar
3 tablespoons cornstarch
1 teaspoon lemon juice
2 packages (3 ounces each) cream cheese
4 tablespoons cream
1 9-inch baked pie shell

1. Wash and hull strawberries. Drain well. Take 1 cup of the smallest, least pretty berries and place in a saucepan with the water and simmer 5 minutes. Reserve remaining berries.
2. Combine sugar and cornstarch. Stir into cooked berries in saucepan and cook, stirring constantly, until syrup is clear and thick. Stir in lemon juice and cool slightly.
3. Mix together cream cheese and cream until light and fluffy. Spread cheese over bottom of baked pie shell.
4. Place reserved whole berries on top of cream cheese. Pour thickened syrup over top of berries.
5. Chill well before serving.
6. Makes one 9-inch pie.

PEACH PIE

1 recipe pastry
¼ to ½ cup sugar
¼ cup flour or 3 tablespoons quick-cooking tapioca
½ teaspoon cinnamon
Dash of nutmeg
6 cups peeled, sliced fresh peaches
1 tablespoon lemon juice
Butter or margarine

1. Heat oven to 450°F.
2. Line a 9-inch pie pan with a little more than half the pastry.
3. Combine sugar, flour, cinnamon, nutmeg and peaches. Place in crust. Sprinkle with lemon juice and dot with butter.
4. Roll remaining pastry out and use for top crust over peaches. Or pastry can be cut into fancy shapes and placed on top of peaches. Flute edges of pie.
5. Bake 15 minutes. Reduce heat to 375°F. Bake 35 to 45 minutes or until crust is golden brown and peaches are tender.
6. Makes one 9-inch pie.

LATTICE-TOP CHERRY PIE

1 recipe pastry
2½ to 3 tablespoons quick-cooking tapioca
1 cup sugar
⅛ teaspoon salt
2 cans (No. 2) pitted red sour cherries, water packed, drained
½ cup reserved cherry juice
1 tablespoon butter or margarine

1. Heat oven to 425°F.
2. Line a 9-inch pie pan with half of the pastry.
3. Combine tapioca, sugar, salt, cherries and juice. Fill pie shell with cherry mixture. Dot with butter or margarine.
4. Roll second half of pastry into a 12-inch circle. Cut into ½-inch strips with a pastry wheel or a sharp knife. Lay 4 or 5 strips loosely across top of filling. Take remaining strips of pastry and weave in basket-weave fashion at right angles to original strips. Trim edges even with pie pan. Press edges down onto bottom crust. Fold under edges. Seal and flute.
5. Bake about 45 minutes or until syrup boils with heavy bubbles that do not burst.
6. Makes one 9-inch pie.

CHOCOLATE CHIFFON PIE

4 cups corn flakes, crushed
2 tablespoons sugar
⅓ cup butter or margarine
1 envelope unflavored gelatin
½ cup sugar
⅛ teaspoon salt
1½ cups milk
1 package (6 ounces) semi-sweet chocolate pieces
1 teaspoon vanilla
1 cup heavy cream, whipped

1. Heat oven to 350°F.
2. Put corn flake crumbs, 2 tablespoons sugar, and butter in a 9-inch pie pan. Place in oven for 5 minutes or until butter is melted. Remove pie pan from oven. Mix well and press mixture evenly and firmly around sides and on bottom of pan. Chill.
3. Mix together gelatine, ½ cup sugar and salt in a saucepan. Stir in milk and semi-sweet chocolate pieces. Cook over medium heat, stirring constantly, until chocolate is melted, about 5 minutes. Remove from heat and beat with a rotary beater until chocolate is blended. Stir in vanilla.
4. Chill, stirring occasionally, until mixture mounds when dropped from a spoon. Fold in whipped cream.
5. Pour mixture into crust. Chill in refrigerator until firm.
6. Before serving, garnish with additional whipped cream, if desired.
7. Makes one 9-inch pie.

PECAN CRUMB PIE

3 medium eggs
1 cup sugar, divided
2 cups graham cracker crumbs
¼ cup flour
1 teaspoon baking powder
½ cup chopped pecans
2 tablespoons butter or margarine, melted
1 teaspoon vanilla
½ cup heavy cream, whipped and sweetened

1. Heat oven to 350°F.
2. Beat eggs until very light with ½ cup of the sugar.
3. Combine remaining sugar with crumbs, flour, baking powder, and pecans. Add butter, vanilla and beaten eggs and mix lightly.
4. Pour into a buttered 9-inch pie pan.
5. Bake 30 to 35 minutes.
6. Cool. Serve with whipped cream.
7. Makes one 9-inch pie.

FROZEN APPLE SOUFFLÉ

4 egg yolks
1 cup sugar
1 envelope unflavored gelatin
⅛ teaspoon salt
1 cup light cream
2 cups canned applesauce
1 teaspoon vanilla
2 cups heavy cream

1. Cut length of foil long enough to go around a 1-quart soufflé dish with some overlap. Fold foil lengthwise and fasten around top of soufflé dish with tape or paper clips to make a 3-inch collar on top of dish.
2. Beat egg yolks in top of a double boiler over hot, not boiling, water until they become very light.
3. Combine sugar, gelatine and salt. Gradually beat into egg yolks.
4. Combine light cream and applesauce in a saucepan and heat. When mixture is hot gradually add to thick egg-yolk mixture, stirring constantly. Continue to cook over hot water, stirring constantly, until mixture is thick and smooth, or until mixture coats a silver spoon.
5. Empty water from bottom of double boiler and fill with ice cubes. Replace top section of double boiler containing cooked mixture and cool over ice, stirring frequently.
6. Add vanilla to cream and whip until stiff. When egg mixture is cooled, fold into whipped cream. Turn mixture into 1-quart soufflé dish with collar.
7. Place in freezer and chill until firm.
8. To serve, remove collar and serve with Ice Cream Rum Sauce.
9. Makes 6 to 8 servings.

ICE CREAM RUM SAUCE

1 pint vanilla ice cream
1 to 2 tablespoons dark rum

1. Soften ice cream and then stir in rum.
2. Serve while it is still creamy soft, before it becomes too liquid.
3. Makes 2 cups sauce.

SPICED PEACHES FLAMBÉ

1 can (1 pound, 13 ounces) peach halves
2 sticks cinnamon, 1 inch long
16 whole cloves
1½ teaspoons cornstarch
1 tablespoon water
2 ounces brandy

1. Drain juice from peaches into a saucepan. Add cinnamon and cloves. Bring to the boiling point.
2. Blend cornstarch with water and add to juice. Cook, stirring constantly, until juice is clear and transparent.
3. Add peaches and heat only until they are hot.
4. Pour mixture into a chafing dish. Ignite burner under chafing dish.
5. Heat brandy in a small saucepan. Pour carefully over peaches. Ignite with a match.
6. Serve as a dessert alone or serve with ice cream.
7. Makes 6 servings.

SYLLABUB DESSERT

½ cup heavy cream
1 tablespoon confectioners' sugar
1 tablespoon brandy
2 oranges, peeled and sectioned
½ cup sliced strawberries

1. Beat heavy cream with a rotary beater just until stiff. Fold in confectioners' sugar and brandy.
2. Layer whipped cream, orange sections and strawberries in parfait glasses.
3. Chill about 30 minutes.
4. Makes 6 servings.

FRESH FRUIT COMPOTE

½ cup light corn syrup
½ cup orange juice
4 whole cloves
⅛ teaspoon ginger
1 tablespoon grated orange rind
1 quart sliced, cubed, or small whole fresh fruit

1. Combine light corn syrup, orange juice, cloves and ginger in a 1½-quart saucepan. Bring to a boil over medium heat and boil 5 minutes.
2. Remove from heat. Remove cloves. Stir in orange rind.
3. Pour over fruit in a serving bowl. Chill well before serving.
4. Makes 4 servings.

APPLESAUCE

1. Wash red cooking apples. Remove stems. Cut apples in chunks. Do not peel and do not core.
2. Put apples into a saucepan.
3. Add 3 ounces water.
4. Put cover on pan with vac-control valve open.
5. Place over medium-high heat.
6. Allow vapor to escape through vac-control valve 3 to 5 minutes.
7. Close vac-control valve and turn off heat. Do not remove cover.
8. Let stand 10 to 15 minutes.
9. Put apples through food press. As the apples are pushed through the food press with the potato masher, the skins and seeds will remain in the food press and the apples will go through.
10. Add sugar to taste to apple sauce.

COOKING TERMS YOU SHOULD KNOW

batter A mixture of flour, liquid, and other ingredients, used as a basis for cake, fritters, coating, or pancakes. Its consistency may range from a thin liquid to a stiff, thick one, depending upon the proportions of the ingredients.

bake To cook in an oven by dry heat; called roasting when applied to meat. In some instances, baking can be done on top of range upside down cake, for example.

baste To moisten food while cooking by spooning on melted fat, pan juices, wine, or other liquids.

beat To mix ingredients together to make a smooth batter with a whisk, spoon, electric mixer, or rotary beater.

beating egg whites To incorporate as much air as possible into the egg whites as you beat, thus increasing their volume. They can be beaten with an electric mixer or rotary beater. Egg whites at room temperature will give more volume than when they are cold.

beating egg whites stiff Egg whites should stand in peaks when beater is lifted from surface, with points of peaks drooping over a bit and surface still moist and glossy.

beating egg whites very stiff Egg whites should stand in peaks, upright without drooping. Surface should look dry.

blend To combine two or more ingredients well, usually with a spoon or electric mixer.

boil To cook food in a boiling liquid in which bubbles constantly rise to the surface and break. In a rapid boil, the bubbles are vigorous and rolling. In a medium boil, the bubbles are gentle. In a very slow boil, the liquid hardly moves and is called a simmer.

braise To brown well on both sides in a little hot fat, then add a small amount of liquid and cook in a tightly covered pan over very low heat until tender.

bread To coat food with dry bread crumbs or cracker crumbs. The food is usually dipped first in a liquid or beaten egg to help the crumbs stick to the surface.

brush on To apply melted fat, salad oil, cream, beaten egg white, or other liquid to the surface of food with a pastry brush or crumpled wax paper.

chill To place in refrigerator or over cracked ice until cold.

chop To cut food into small pieces. Place food to be chopped on a wooden board, hold tip of a French knife close to surface of board with one hand, then move knife handle vigorously up and down on the food with the other hand. Repeat until food is thoroughly chopped.

coat To cover food lightly but thoroughly with either a liquid or a dry substance. To coat with flour, place food and flour in a paper bag and shake thoroughly.

condiment Any seasoning added to food to enhance its flavor.

core To remove the inedible central portion of certain fruits, using a paring knife or corer.

cream To rub or work fat, such as butter, margarine, or fat with sugar with spoon against the sides of a bowl until creamy. Or to use electric mixer until mixture is soft and creamy.

crisp To make firm. Leafy vegetables, such as lettuce, are rinsed in water and then chilled. Dry food, such as bread and crackers, are heated in the oven.

crumb To break into small pieces. Fresh bread crumbs are made by pulling a piece of fresh bread into small, soft particles. Stale bread crumbs are made with dried-out bread by crushing with a rolling pin or in a blender. Refrigerate stale crumbs and use to coat foods.

crush To pulverize by rolling with a rolling pin until the consistency of coarse powder. Fruits are usually crushed by mashing with a potato masher until they lose their shape.

cube To cut into small, equal-sized pieces, about ¼ inch to ½ inch.

cut in To combine solid shortening with flour in pastry making. Using two knives scissor fashion, or a pastry blender, cut shortening into flour or flour mixture until flour-coated fat particles are of desired size.

degrease To remove fat from a liquid. Let the liquid stand for a few minutes so that the fat will rise to the top. Skim the surface with a spoon to collect the fat. Wrap an ice cube in a piece of paper toweling, draw across the surface to soak up any remaining fat. If time permits, refrigerate the liquid in its container until the fat congeals on the surface, thus making it simple to lift off.

dice To cut into very small, even cubes.

dissolve To mix a dry substance with a liquid until it dissolves. Or to combine a dry substance with a liquid and heating it until it melts, as with gelatin.

dot To scatter small bits of butter or margarine over the surface of food.

drain To remove liquid, usually by allowing food to go through a colander or strainer until the liquid has dripped off, as when draining spaghetti. Or by tipping pan and holding lid in place so that just the liquid is poured off.

dredge To coat food wth flour, sugar, bread, or cracker crumbs.

drippings Fat or juices that cook out of meat or poultry during the cooking process.

fillet A strip of lean, boneless meat or fish.

fold To incorporate a delicate mixture into a thicker, heavier one, such as folding in beaten egg whites or whipped cream. Place egg white or cream on top of mixture. Pass a rubber spatula down through mixture and across bottom of pan or bowl; bring up some of the mixture and place on top of egg whites or cream. Repeat until egg whites or cream are evenly combined with heavier mixture. This should be a quick but gentle operation, to keep in as much of the beaten air as possible.

fry To cook in a very small amount of hot fat or oil.

goulash A thick hungarian meat and vegetable stew, usually flavored with paprika.

grate To rub food on a grater to produce fine, medium, or coarse particles. When grating lemon rind, use only the colored part of the rind.

grease To rub butter, margarine, shortening, or salad oil lightly on the surface of food or utensils.

julienne Food cut into thin, matchlike strips.

knead To work dough by pressing it with the heels of the hands, folding, turning and pressing, usually applied to yeast dough and worked on a floured board. Yeast dough should be kneaded until it looks full and rounded, smooth, satiny, and tightly stretched.

lard To lay strips of salt pork or bacon on top of meat or to make incisions or gashes in the meat and force fat into the gashes. This prevents meat from drying out and makes it self-basting while it is cooking.

marinate To let food stand in a seasoned liquid to enhance its flavor or to make it more tender.

mash To soften and break down food by using a masher, the back of a spoon, a fork, or by forcing food through a press.

melt To change fat, like butter or margarine, into a liquid state by heating.

mince To cut or chop very fine with a chopper or knife.

mound A spoonful of a mixture which is dropped onto another mixture. A mound forms a definite heap and does not blend into the original mixture.

pare To remove the outer covering of a fruit or vegetable with a knife or a paring tool.

pit To remove seeds or stones from fruit.

poach To cook food immersed in a liquid that is barely simmering.

preheat To heat an oven or boiler to the desired baking temperature before putting in the food to be cooked.

rind The outer skin of fruits and vegetables. Grated orange and lemon rinds are frequently used in cooking.

sauté To cook food in a small amount of hot fat or salad oil in a skillet. This is usually done briefly to brown food before cooking by some other method.

scald To heat a liquid to just under the boiling point, as when a recipe calls for scalded milk. It also means to pour boiling water over food.

score To make shallow slits or gashes on the surface of food with a knife or a fork.

separate To separate egg yolks from the whites.

set A condition in which liquids have congealed and retain their shape, usually referring to gelatin mixtures.

shred To cut or break into thin pieces.

sift To put through a flour sifter or fine sieve, usually referring to flour or confectioners' sugar.

simmer To cook just below the boiling temperature.

skewer To hold foods in place by means of metal or wooden skewers.

skim To remove a substance, usually fat, from the surface of a liquid.

sliver To cut or split into long thin pieces.

steam To cook by steam rising from a liquid.

stew A thick combination of various foods cooked in liquid at a low temperature for a long period of time.

stir To blend with circular motion using a spoon, widening the circles until all the ingredients are well mixed.

stock A liquid in which meat, poultry, fish, bones, or vegetables and seasonings have been cooked.

thicken To make a liquid more dense by adding flour, cornstarch, or egg yolks.

toast To brown in a broiler, oven, toaster, or over hot coals.

toss To mix lightly with two forks or a fork and spoon. Used in referring to salads or in mixtures where the food should be handled gently and not broken up.

truss To arrange poultry for cooking by binding the wings and legs.

unmold To remove food from a mold. Dip a small pointed knife in warm water and run it around inner edges of the mold. Dip mold just to rim in warm water for 2 to 3 seconds. Remove and shake gently to loosen gelatin. Cover top of mold with chilled inverted serving plate. Invert plate and mold together. Lift off mold carefully. If the contents stick, rub the mold gently with a hot damp towel. If necessary, repeat entire process.

whip To beat rapidly, usually with an electric mixer or rotary beater, to incorporate air and increase volume, as with egg whites or cream.

A Word About Baking

Following the recipe exactly is essential for successful baking. You will learn that you can adjust ingredients and seasonings to your own taste when making stews and soups, but every direction in the recipe must be followed when baking. Baking troubles can usually be traced to one of three basic causes: (1) not using the ingredients called for; (2) not using standard measurements; and (3) not baking in the right pan at the right temperature.

INGREDIENTS

FLOUR   In the cake, cookie, and bread recipes in this book, we indicate the kind of flour to be used. Never substitute another kind. All-purpose flour is an all-around type flour. It comes in bags and gives good results in baking and for other uses such as sauces and gravies. Self-rising flour is an all-purpose or cake flour to which leavening and salt have been added. Use only in recipes that call for self-rising flour. Cake flour comes in packages and is milled and refined especially for cakes. Instant-type flours are generally refined all-purpose flours that have a finer consistency than all-purpose flour and pour like sugar or salt. They perform differently in cooking so should not be substituted in general baking. However, they work well for making gravies and cream sauces. Other flours, such as whole wheat and rye flour, are used mostly in baking bread. Do not sift these before using.

LEAVENING AGENTS   There are three kinds of baking powder, and each acts differently. Double-acting baking powder reacts very slowly, releasing about a third of its leavening in the cold mixture and the remainder in the heat of the oven. Phosphate baking powder reacts slowly and requires heat to liberate its leavening action. Tartrate baking powder reacts rapidly and begins its action at room temperature as soon as a liquid is added. Double-acting baking powder is the most widely available and the most widely used. Check each recipe for the type used.

Baking soda is used alone or with baking powder to leaven cakes made with buttermilk, sour milk, chocolate, molasses, and fruit juices. The acid from these ingredients reacts with the soda to release leavening. When using baking soda, don't delay mixing or baking too long.

CHOCOLATE AND COCOA   Unsweetened chocolate comes in wrapped squares weighing 1 ounce each, eight squares in each package. It also comes in little foil packets, pre-melted. It is pure chocolate, a special blend of finest cocoa beans. Semi-sweet chocolate pieces come in 6-ounce and 12-ounce bags. Use as is in recipes which call for chocolate pieces. Melt over hot, not boiling water. German sweet cooking chocolate comes in ¼-pound bars and is used for cooking and eating. Cocoa is prepared from cocoa beans by removing varying amounts of the cocoa butter. Different brands have different flavors, so try several.

SUGAR   Granulated white sugar, made from either sugar beets or sugar cane is the general all-purpose sugar. Superfine sugar has a finer consistency and is used occasionally in baking and in drinks. Confectioner's or powdered sugar is a very finely pulverized sugar with a small amount of cornstarch added. It is used in making frostings and for dusting cakes and cookies. Brown sugar gets its color from its molasses content. Light brown sugar has a delicate molasses flavor, while dark brown sugar has more molasses flavor. Granulated brown sugar has been refined in a free-flowing form. Don't substitute it in recipes without consulting substitution chart on package.

MEASURING

FLOUR   Before measuring, sift it once onto a square of waxed paper. Spoon sifted flour lightly into a graduated metal measuring cup until flour is piled over top of cup. Level off with edge of spatula or knife. Do not pack down or tap cup.

DRY INGREDIENTS   Baking powder, soda, and salt are measured by dipping spoon of specified size into dry ingredient until it overflows. Level off with edge of knife or spatula. Spoon granulated sugar lightly into a graduated metal measuring cup; level off with edge of knife or spatula. Spoon brown sugar into a graduated metal measuring cup, packing it down with the back of a spoon just enough so that it holds its shape when turned out.

LIQUIDS   Use a glass measuring cup with rim above the 1-cup line. Set cup on level surface. Lower head so measuring is done at eye level, then fill cup to the desired mark.

SOLID SHORTENINGS   Pack firmly into a graduated metal measuring cup; level off with edge of knife or spatula. When butter or margarine is wrapped in quarter-pound sticks, each stick measures ½ cup or 8 tablespoons.

A TABLE OF EQUIVALENTS

FOOD	WEIGHT	EQUIVALENT
Almonds, unshelled, whole	1 pound	1¾ cups nutmeats
Almonds, blanched, whole	1 pound	3½ cups nutmeats
Apples	1 pound	3½ cups pared and sliced
Bananas	1 pound (3 medium)	2½ cups sliced
Berries	1 quart	3½ cups
Bread	1 slice	¼ to ⅓ cup dry crumbs
Bread	1 slice	¾ to 1 cup soft crumbs
Butter or margarine	1 pound	2 cups
Candied Fruit and Peels	1 pound	3 cups, cut up
Cheese, Cheddar	½ pound	2 cups grated
Cheese, cottage	½ pound	1 cup
Cheese, cream	3-ounce package	6 tablespoons
Coffee, ground	1 pound	40 to 45 serving cups of coffee
Crackers, graham	15	1 cup fine crumbs
Crackers, soda	22	1 cup fine crumbs
Cream, heavy	½ pint	2 cups whipped
Dates	1 pound	2 cups pitted
Egg Whites	8 to 11	1 cup
Egg Yolks	12 to 16	1 cup
Flour, all-purpose	1 pound	4 cups sifted
Flour, cake	1 pound	3¾ to 4 cups sifted
Gelatin	¼-ounce package	1 tablespoon
Lemon	1 medium	3 tablespoons juice
Lemon Rind	1 medium	1 tablespoon grated rind
Milk, evaporated	14½-ounce can	1⅔ cups
Milk, sweetened, condensed	14-ounce can	1¼ cups
Noodles	1 cup uncooked	2 cups cooked
Orange	1 medium	⅓ cup juice
Orange rind	1 medium	2 tablespoons grated rind
Peanuts, unshelled	1 pound	2 to 2½ cups nutmeats
Pecans, unshelled	1 pound	2¼ cups nutmeats
Raisins	1 pound	3 cups
Rice	1 cup raw	3 cups cooked
Spaghetti	1 pound uncooked	7 cups cooked
Sugar, brown	1 pound	2¼ to 2⅓ cups, firmly packed
Sugar, confectioners'	1 pound	About 4 cups sifted
Sugar, granulated	1 pound	2½ cups
Walnuts, unshelled	1 pound	1⅔ cups nutmeats

EQUIVALENT MEASURES

⅓ of ½ teaspoon	pinch
½ of ¼ teaspoon	⅛ teaspoon
3 teaspoons	1 tablespoon
2 tablespoons	⅛ cup
4 tablespoons	¼ cup
5 tablespoons plus 1 teaspoon	⅓ cup
8 tablespoons	½ cup
12 tablespoons	¾ cup
16 tablespoons	1 cup
1 cup	8 fluid ounces
2 cups	1 pint
2 pints	1 quart
1 quart	4 cups
4 quarts	1 gallon
1 pound	16 ounces (dry measure)

A WORD ABOUT CANS

Be a label reader when it comes time to shop. Can labels give a variety of information such as grade of product, what is in the can if it is a mixture, and most important when following recipes, the size of the can and how much it contains. Here is a chart to help you, just in case all information is not available on the can.

INDUSTRY TERM	APPROXIMATE NET WEIGHT OR FLUID MEASURE	APPROXIMATE CUPS OR SERVINGS
6 ounces	6 ounces	¾ cup
8 ounces	8 ounces	1 cup 2 servings
Picnic	10½ to 12 ounces	1¼ cups 3 servings
12 ounces	12 ounces	1½ cups 3-4 servings
No. 300	14 to 16 ounces	1¾ cups 3-4 servings
No. 303	16 to 17 ounces	2 cups 4 servings
No. 2	1 pound 4 ounces or 1 pint 2 ounces	2½ cups 5 servings
No. 2½	1 pound 13 ounces	3½ cups 7 servings
No. 3	3 pounds 3 ounces	5¾ cups 10 to 12 servings
46 fluid ounces	1 quart 14 fluid ounces	5¾ cups 10 to 12 servings

BEEF CHART

RETAIL CUTS OF BEEF—WHERE THEY COME FROM AND HOW TO COOK THEM

CHUCK
Braise, Cook in Liquid

- ②③ Inside Chuck Roll
- ⑤⑥ Chuck Short Ribs
- ② Chuck Tender
- ③ Petite Steaks*
- ②③ Blade Pot-roast or Steak
- ④⑤ Arm Pot-roast or Steak
- ⑤ Boneless Shoulder Pot-roast or Steak
- ⑥ Boston Cut

RIB
Roast, Broil, Panbroil, Panfry

- ② Standing Rib Roast
- ② Rib Steak
- ② Rib Steak, Boneless
- ② Delmonico (Rib Eye) Roast or Steak

SHORT LOIN
Roast, Broil, Panbroil, Panfry

- ① Club Steak
- ② T-Bone Steak
- ③ Porterhouse Steak
- ①②③ Top Loin Steak
- ②③ Filet Mignon Tenderloin Steak (also from Sirloin 1, 2, 3)

SIRLOIN
Roast, Broil, Panbroil, Panfry

- ① Pin Bone Sirloin Steak
- ② Flat Bone Sirloin Steak
- ③ Wedge Bone Sirloin Steak
- ①②③ Boneless Sirloin Steak

ROUND
Braise, Cook in Liquid

- ③ Round Steak
- ① Standing Rump*
- ③ Top Round Steak*
- ① Rolled Rump*
- ③ Outside (Bottom) Round Steak or Pot-roast
- ③ Eye of Round
- ④ Heel of Round

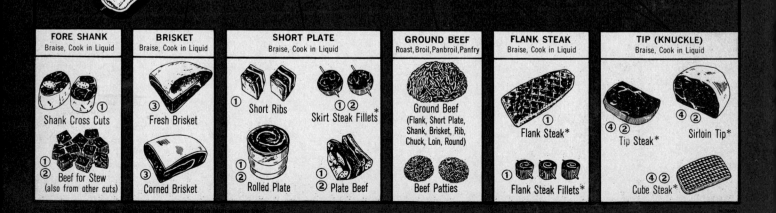

FORE SHANK
Braise, Cook in Liquid

- ① Shank Cross Cuts
- ①② Beef for Stew (also from other cuts)

BRISKET
Braise, Cook in Liquid

- ③ Fresh Brisket
- ③ Corned Brisket

SHORT PLATE
Braise, Cook in Liquid

- ① Short Ribs
- ①② Skirt Steak Fillets*
- ①② Rolled Plate
- ② Plate Beef

GROUND BEEF
Roast, Broil, Panbroil, Panfry

- Ground Beef (Flank, Short Plate, Shank, Brisket, Rib, Chuck, Loin, Round)
- Beef Patties

FLANK STEAK
Braise, Cook in Liquid

- ① Flank Steak*
- ① Flank Steak Fillets*

TIP (KNUCKLE)
Braise, Cook in Liquid

- ④② Tip Steak*
- ④② Sirloin Tip*
- ④② Cube Steak*

NATIONAL LIVESTOCK AND MEAT BOARD

PORK CHART

RETAIL CUTS OF PORK — WHERE THEY COME FROM AND HOW TO COOK THEM

Boston Butt

Rolled Boston Butt
Roast

Blade Steak
Braise, Panfry

Smoked Shoulder Butt
Roast (bake), Cook in Liquid, Broil, Panbroil, Panfry

Sausage *
Panfry, Braise, Bake

Porklet
Braise, Panfry

Fat Back
Panfry, Cook in Liquid

Lard
Pastry, Cookies, Quick Breads, Cakes, Frying

Blade Loin Roast

Center Loin Roast
Roast

Rolled Loin Roast

Sirloin Roast

Tenderloin
Roast, Braise, Panfry

Back Ribs
Roast (bake), Braise, Cook in Liquid

Rib Chop

Loin Chop

Sirloin Chop

Butterfly Chop

Braise, Broil, Panfry

Blade Chop

Top Loin Chop

Smoked Loin Chop
Broil, Panfry

Country Style Backbone

Canadian Style Bacon
Roast, Broil, Panbroil, Panfry

Smoked Ham Shank Portion

Smoked Ham Butt Portion
Roast (bake), Cook in Liquid

Rolled Fresh Ham (leg)

Smoked Ham Boneless Roll
Roast (bake)

Canned Ham
Roast, (bake)

Sliced Cooked "Boiled" Ham

Smoked Ham Center Slice
Broil, Panbroil, Panfry

Jowl Bacon
Cook in Liquid, Broil, Panbroil, Panfry

Pig's Feet
Cook in Liquid, Braise

Fresh Hock

Smoked Hock
Braise — Cook in Liquid

Arm Roast
Roast

Fresh Picnic
Roast

Smoked Picnic
Roast (bake), Cook in Liquid

Canned Luncheon Meat *
Roast (bake), Broil, Panbroil

Arm Steak
Braise, Panfry

Rolled Fresh Picnic
Roast

Canned Picnic
Roast, (bake)

Salt Pork
Broil, Panbroil, Panfry, Cook in Liquid, Bake

Spareribs
Roast (bake), Braise, Cook in Liquid

Sliced Bacon

Slab Bacon
Broil, Panbroil, Panfry, Bake

LAMB CHART

RETAIL CUTS OF LAMB — WHERE THEY COME FROM AND HOW TO COOK THEM

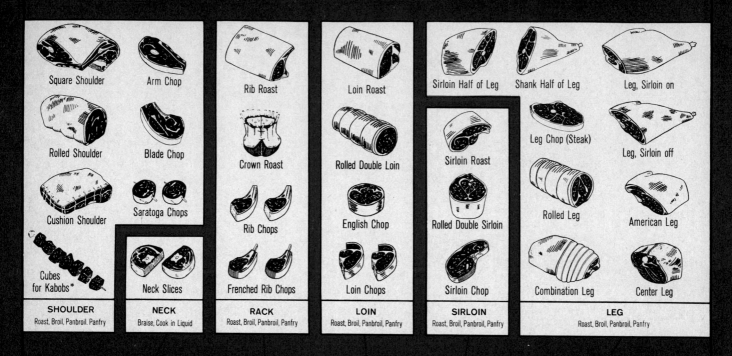

SHOULDER	NECK	RACK	LOIN	SIRLOIN	LEG
Roast, Broil, Panbroil, Panfry	Braise, Cook in Liquid	Roast, Broil, Panbroil, Panfry	Roast, Broil, Panbroil, Panfry	Roast, Broil, Panbroil, Panfry	Roast, Broil, Panbroil, Panfry

Square Shoulder · Arm Chop · Rolled Shoulder · Blade Chop · Cushion Shoulder · Saratoga Chops · Cubes for Kabobs* · Neck Slices · Rib Roast · Crown Roast · Rib Chops · Frenched Rib Chops · Loin Roast · Rolled Double Loin · English Chop · Loin Chops · Sirloin Roast · Rolled Double Sirloin · Sirloin Chop · Sirloin Half of Leg · Shank Half of Leg · Leg, Sirloin on · Leg Chop (Steak) · Leg, Sirloin off · Rolled Leg · American Leg · Combination Leg · Center Leg

FORE SHANK	BREAST	HIND SHANK	GROUND OR CUBED LAMB
Braise, Cook in Liquid	Roast, Braise, Broil, Panbroil, Panfry, Cook in Liquid	Braise, Cook in Liquid	Roast, Broil, Panbroil, Panfry, Braise, Cook in Liquid

Fore Shank · Breast · Rolled Breast · Stuffed Breast · Hind Shank · Lamb for Stew* (Large Pieces) (Small Pieces) · Riblets · Ribs (for Barbecue, etc.) · Brisket Pieces · Stuffed Chops · Cube Steak* · Ground Lamb* · Lamburgers*

*LAMB FOR STEW, GRINDING OR CUBING MAY COME FROM ANY WHOLESALE CUT

NATIONAL LIVE STOCK AND MEAT BOARD

VEAL CHART

RETAIL CUTS OF VEAL — WHERE THEY COME FROM AND HOW TO COOK THEM

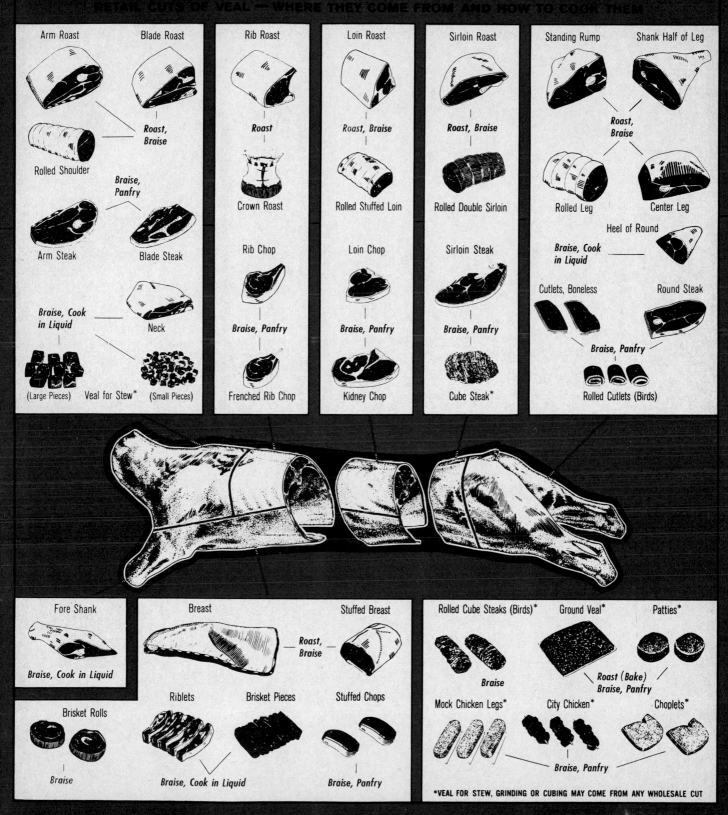

Arm Roast

Blade Roast

Rolled Shoulder

Roast, Braise

Braise, Panfry

Arm Steak

Blade Steak

Braise, Cook in Liquid

Neck

(Large Pieces)   Veal for Stew*   (Small Pieces)

Rib Roast

Roast

Crown Roast

Rib Chop

Braise, Panfry

Frenched Rib Chop

Loin Roast

Roast, Braise

Rolled Stuffed Loin

Loin Chop

Braise, Panfry

Kidney Chop

Sirloin Roast

Roast, Braise

Rolled Double Sirloin

Sirloin Steak

Braise, Panfry

Cube Steak*

Standing Rump

Shank Half of Leg

Roast, Braise

Rolled Leg

Center Leg

Heel of Round

Braise, Cook in Liquid

Cutlets, Boneless

Round Steak

Braise, Panfry

Rolled Cutlets (Birds)

Fore Shank

Braise, Cook in Liquid

Brisket Rolls

Braise

Breast

Roast, Braise

Stuffed Breast

Riblets

Brisket Pieces

Braise, Cook in Liquid

Stuffed Chops

Braise, Panfry

Rolled Cube Steaks (Birds)*

Ground Veal*

Patties*

Braise

Roast (Bake) Braise, Panfry

Mock Chicken Legs*

City Chicken*

Choplets*

Braise, Panfry

*VEAL FOR STEW, GRINDING OR CUBING MAY COME FROM ANY WHOLESALE CUT

INDEX

Roast	. . . .	52
Ribs of Beef	. . . .	52
Steak		
Chinese Pepper	. . . .	55
Diane	. . . .	53
Oriental Chuck	. . . .	54
Round Steak Birds	. . . . . .	54
Round Steak Stronganoff	. . . . .	55
Stuffed Flank	. . . . . .	54
Swiss	. . . .	53
Stew		
Barbados	. . . .	60
Bavarian	. . . .	56
Meat Balls	. . . . . .	58
Old Fashioned	. . . . . .	56
Rancher Supper	. . . . .	61
Swiss	. . . .	57

ARTICHOKES **25**
 Fried 25
 Hearts with Mushrooms 25
 Lobster Artichoke Bake 98

ASPARAGUS **25**
 Vinaigrette Bundles 26

BACON
 Pan-Broiled 64

BEANS, Dried
 Chili 57
 Lima Bean Soup 91
 Quebec Green Pea Soup 91
 Split Pea Soup 91

BEANS, GREEN **26**
 and Mushrooms 27
 Dutch 26
 Herbed 27
 Italiano 28
 Peppered 26
 Piquant 27
 Savory 27
 Viennese Snap 27

BEANS, LIMA **34**
 Parmesan 34
 Pimiento 34

BEEF
 Chinese, and Vegetables 60
 Corned and Cabbage 61
 Creamy 60
 Fondue Bourguignonne 86
 Goulash
 Beef 60
 Hungarian 56
 Hamburger
 Beef Balls Casserole 59
 Burgundy Beef Balls 58
 Chili 57
 Meat Balls and Spaghetti 12
 Meat Balls Del Vino 58
 Sour Cream Sauce Burgers . . . 56
 Swedish Meat Balls 59
 Wine-Mushroom Hamburgers . . . 57
 Meat Loaf 57
 Mount Vernon Short Ribs 55
 Pot Roast 52
 Barbecued 60
 Geoff's 52
 Sauerbraten 53
 Sweet and Sour 59

BEETS **28**
 Harvard 29
 in Orange Sauce 28
 with Claret Sauce 28

BREADS, QUICK
 Baking Powder Biscuits 101
 Banana Walnut 105
 Batter Rolls 102
 Coffee Cake 102
 Date Nut Loaf 105
 Easy Danish Kringle 103
 Garlic 105
 Muffins 101
 Orange Honey Cubes 105
 Parsley Buttered 105
 Popovers 104
 Quick Caramel Buns 103
 Sherried Coffee Cake 102
 Sour Cream Biscuits 101

BROCCOLI **29**
 Indienne 29
 with Sour Cream Sauce 29

BRUSSELS SPROUTS **29**
 Caraway 29
 Golden Nugget 30

CABBAGE **30**
 Dutch 30
 Norwegian 30

CAFE BRULOT DIABOLIQUE **86**

CAKES
 Banana Nut 107
 Elegant Walnut Devil's Food 110
 Fancy 110
 Gingerpeach Upside-Down 110
 Pineapple Skillet 107

CARROTS **30**
 Cranberry 31
 Glazed 31
 Pan Glazed 31
 Parsley 31
 Tangy Glazed 31

CAULIFLOWER **32**
 and Tomatoes 32
 Cheesed 32
 Flowerets 32
 Whole 32

CELERY **32**
 Braised 33
 Sweet and Sour 33

CHICKEN

A la Valee d'Auge 76
Breast with Almonds 78
Chop Suey 76
Cold Curried Soup 92
Con Limon 79
Country Captain 79
Curried Orange 78
Fried 77
      New Pan-Fried 75
Hawaiian 77
Lemon 77
Pirate Creole 78
Quick Chick Creole 76
Roast 75
Rose's Party 83
Stroganoff 76
Tarragon 77
Veronique 79
with Tomato and Avocado 78

COOKIES

Almond Butter Crisps 113
Black-Eyed Susans 113
Butter Nut Wafers 112
Chocolate Chip Cookies 112
Mexican Tea Cakes 113
Peanut Butter Cookies 112
Refrigerator Cookies 113
Saucepan Brownies 112

CORN **33**

Mexican 33
Pudding 33

DESSERTS

Applesauce 117
Fondue Chocolat 86
Fresh Fruit Compote 116
Frozen Apple Souffle 116
Orange Blossom 83
Spiced Peaches Flambe 116
Syllabub 116

DUCK

Mandarin 81

EGGPLANT **33**

Moussaka 34

EGGS

Baked 15
Benedict 16
Cheese Soufflé 17
Creamed 16
Fried 15
Hard Cooked 15
Kay's Casserole 17
Omelet, Puffy Cheese 16
Poached 15
      Mushroom Poached 16
Scrambled 15
Shrimp Egg-Foo-Yong 17
Soft-cooked 15

FISH

Fillet Puffs 98
Oven-Fried Steaks 99
Perch Almondine 97
Seafood Newburg 97
Steaks in Wine sauce 99
Tomato Fillets 99

HAM

Baked 64
Casserole 11

ICING AND TOPPING

Fluffy Cream Cheese Icing 110
Sherry Cinnamon Topping 102

LAMB

and Barley Soup 93
Braised Shoulder 68
Casserole 66
Chilindron 67
Chops
      and Leeks 65
      Peruvian 65
      Sherried 65
Cottage Pie 68
Roast Leg of 65
Shanks 68
      Braised with Vegetables 66
Stew 66
      Irish 68
      Italian and Bean 67
Stuffed Peppers 67

LASAGNA

California 13
Quick 13

LOBSTER

Artichoke Bake 98
Baked 95
Boiled 95
Cantonese 95
Cheese and 97
Shrimp Thermidor 98

MACARONI

Baked and Cheese 9
Family Favorite 9
Mountaineers' and Tuna 10
Pork Casserole 9

MEAT

Braising 50
Cooking in liquid 50
Know How 43
Pan Broiling 49
Pan Frying 50
Top Stove Roasting 43

MUSHROOMS **35**

Broiled 35
Italian Style 35
Stuffed 35

NOODLES

Chipped Beef and, Casserole 11
Company Casserole 10
Egg, Bake 10
Green, en Coquille 12
Ham Casserole 11
Turkey-Ham Casserole 10

ONIONS **35**

Creamed, and Peas Sauterne 36
Green 36
Sunny Baked 36

PEAS **36**

Creamed, and Mushrooms 37
Parisienne 37

PIZZA

Cheese	104
Dough	103
Mushroom Hamburger	104
Shrimp and Pepper	103
Wagon Wheel	104

PIE

Chocolate Chiffon	115
Lattice-Top Cherry	115
Pastry	114
Peach	115
Pecan Crumb	115
Strawberry Glaze	114

PORK

Chops	
Dixie	62
Orange Ginger	62
Stuffed	62
in Orange-Mustard Sauce	64
Loin of Pork	62
Savory Pork Pie	64
Spare Ribs	
Baked Stuffed	63
Barbecued	63
Sweet and Pungent	63

POTATOES, WHITE — **37**

Baked	37
Cheddar Scalloped	37
Cooked	37
Hashed Brown	38
in Cream	38
Pancakes	38
Scalloped	38
Venetian	38

POTATOES, SWEET OR YAMS — **40**

Baked in Marmalade Wine Sauce	40
Candied	40

ROCK CORNISH GAME HENS — **79**

SAUCES

Béarnaise	86
Ice Cream Rum	116
Smitane	86
Spaghetti	12
Quick Hollandaise	16

SCALLOPS

Creamed	99
Pan-Sauteed	99
Saucy	97

SHRIMP

Boiled	96
Curry	83
Italian	96
Lobster, Thermidor	98
Marinara	98
Supper, and Rice	96
Sweet and Pungent	96

SPAGHETTI

Fettucine Alla Roman	13
Meat Balls	12
Rosy	12
Sauce	12
Sausage Casserole	13
Turkey Tetrazzini	11

SOUPS

Cheese and Onion	90
Cold Cucumber Soup	92
Cold Curried Chicken	92
Cold Curried Cream of Vegetable	92
Corn Chowder	93
Creme de Pourri	91
Down East Fish Chowder	93
Hamburger	90
Hearty Vegetable	90
Lamb and Barley	93
Lima Bean	91
Minestrone a la Milanese	89
New England Clam Chowder	93
Quebec Green Pea Soup	91
Quick Minestrone	89
Speedy Gazpacho	90
Split Pea Soup	91
Turkey Soup	92
Vegetable Bean-Pot	92

SPINACH — **38**

Spinach Timbales	39

SQUASH — **39**

Stuffed Acorn	39

SQUASH, SUMMER — **39**

Fried Zucchini	40
with Sour Cream	40

STUFFING

Butter Chicken	75
Corn Bread and Sausage	81
Old Fashioned	80

TOMATOES — **41**

Broiled, Provencal	41
Fried	41

TURKEY

Curry	81
Gravy	80
Ham Casserole	10
Quick Turkey Divan	81
Roast	80
Soup	92
Tetrazzini	11
Thawing	80

TURNIPS AND RUTABAGAS — **41**

Glazed	41

VEAL

and Mushrooms on Curried Rice	71
and Peppers	70
Birds	71
Blanquette of Veal	70
Braised Shoulder	69
Breast, with Mushroom Stuffing	72
Chops All in One	69
Cutlets, Oriental	69
Italian	70
Parmigiano	72
Party Veal Pot Roast	69
Rice-Stuffed Veal Rolls	72
Sautéed Calf's Liver	73
Scallops, Marsala	73
Scallops with Lemon	71
Spicy, Pot Roast	70
Stew	73
Stew with Dumplings	73

VEGETABLES

Before Cooking	19
Canned	22
Care of Fresh	19
Cooking Fresh	19
Cooking Frozen	22
Frozen	22
Great Go Togethers	23
Seasoning	23

YAMS — **40**

Baked in Marmalade-Wine Sauce	40

Form No. 5-5097

REGISTRATION CERTIFICATE   № 220819

Please register my new cookware set in my name. I have examined the complete set and find it exactly as I have ordered. I understand that it is fully covered as specified in Vollrath's 50 year guarantee.

DATE _____

NAME _____

ADDRESS _____

CITY _____ STATE _____ ZIP _____

Purchased From _____

COMMENTS ON MY NEW STAINLESS STEEL COOKWARE:

_____
_____
_____
_____

I HAVE RECEIVED SEVERAL COMPLIMENTS FROM FRIENDS AND RELATIVES ON MY BEAUTIFUL, NEW STAINLESS STEEL COOKWARE. I SUGGEST YOU SHOW IT TO THE PERSONS LISTED BELOW, WITHOUT OBLIGATION ON THEIR PART.

NAME _____

ADDRESS _____

CITY _____ STATE _____ ZIP _____

NAME _____

ADDRESS _____

CITY _____ STATE _____ ZIP _____

NAME _____

ADDRESS _____

CITY _____ STATE _____ ZIP _____

REPLACEMENT HANDLE ORDER FORM

To order replacement handles simply circle the illustrations matching your set, indicate quantity desired, and send this card with your remittance to: **The Vollrath Co., Customer Service Dept., P. O. Box 611, Sheboygan, WI 53081.**

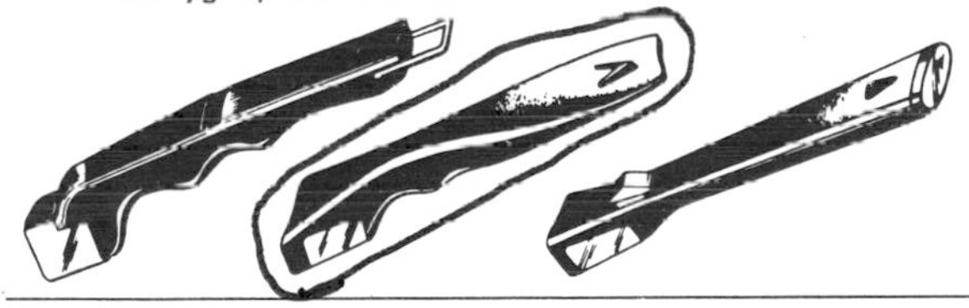

QUANTITY_____
LONG HANDLES
@ $1.50 EACH

QUANTITY_____
SIDE HANDLES
@ $1.00 EACH

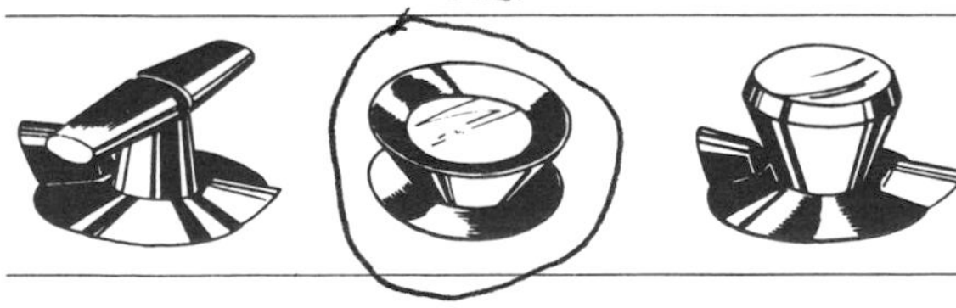

QUANTITY_____
COVER KNOBS
@ $1.00 EACH

AMOUNT ENCLOSED _____

NAME _____

ADDRESS _____

CITY _____ STATE _____ ZIP _____

INCOME OPPORTUNITY!

Would you or do you know someone who would like to earn $50 or $60 a week part time or begin a rewarding, exciting career as a fulltime cookware sales dealer? Please send complete information without obligation to:

NAME _____

ADDRESS _____

CITY _____ STATE _____ ZIP

INTERESTED IN: ☐ Full Time   ☐ Part Time

Area Preferred _____

☐ Can Relocate

Vollrath — SINCE 1874 —

1236 N. 18th STREET
SHEBOYGAN, WISCONSIN 53081

Attn: Sandra Vee
Customer Service Division

Vollrath SINCE 1874

1236 N. 18th STREET
SHEBOYGAN, WISCONSIN 53081

Attn: National Sales Manager

Part No. 08066-1057   Printed in U.S.A.

50 Year Guarantee

STAINLESS STEEL COOKING UTENSILS

This Guarantee is backed by the integrity of our Company and all of our resources. All Vollrath Cooking Utensils are guaranteed to be free from defects in material, construction, and workmanship when shipped to the customer.

We guarantee each utensil to be constructed of 304 stainless steel. All handle attachments are electrically welded to the utensil. Each utensil designed for use over direct heat is constructed of two layers of stainless steel between which is bonded a layer of special heat conducting metal. Covers, casseroles, and steamers are constructed of heavy weight, single sheet stainless steel. These utensils do not need a heat conducting core.

Vollrath guarantees its Stainless Steel Cooking Utensils against rusting, corrosion, chipping, peeling or wearing off in normal household use. Any piece that does so should be returned, prepaid, directly to The Vollrath Company, 1236 North 18th Street, Sheboygan, Wisconsin 53081 for replacement. Any handle bracket on pan or screw on cover which breaks loose from the utensils or covers will be repaired without charge if returned prepaid to our factory. If it is not possible to repair the piece damaged it will be replaced without charge.

All handles and knobs on your Stainless Steel Cookware are made of solid bakelite which is practically indestructible. However, under certain conditions they will break. Handles and knobs cannot be replaced after use without charge. A replacement charge of $1.50 is made for each saucepan handle; $1.00 for each side handle or cover knob. Any handles or knobs broken in shipment will be replaced at no charge.

Casualty warranty. . . . We guarantee to replace your entire Set of Stainless Steel Cookware (or any part thereof) at one-half the then current retail price at such time if it is accidentally lost, stolen, destroyed, or damaged by fire, flood, storm or earthquake . . . or misuse. Proof of loss must be submitted to The Vollrath Company, 1236 North 18th Street, Sheboygan, Wisconsin 53081 within 60 days of its occurrence.

This Guarantee, of necessity, is subject to any government restriction or circumstances beyond our control.

THE VOLLRATH COMPANY
1236 North 18th Street
Sheboygan, Wisconsin 53081